The COOKIE BOOK

DECADENT BITES *for* EVERY OCCASION

REBECCA FIRTH

**CREATOR OF
DISPLACEDHOUSEWIFE**

PAGE STREET
PUBLISHING CO.

PAGE STREET
PUBLISHING CO.

First published in 2018 by
Page Street Publishing Co.
27 Congress Street, Suite 105
Salem, MA 01970
www.pagestreetpublishing.com

Distributed by Macmillan, sales in Canada by The Canadian Manda Group.

22 21 20 19 18   2 3 4 5 6

ISBN-13: 978-1-62414-637-4
ISBN-10: 1-62414-637-6

Library of Congress Control Number: 2018932226

Cover and book design by Meg Baskis for Page Street Publishing Co.
Photography by Rebecca Firth
Author photo by Christine Carlson

Printed and bound in the United States

Page Street Publishing protects our planet by donating to nonprofits like The Trustees, which focuses on local land conservation.

To Stella and Gavin . . .

YOU'LL ALWAYS BE MY FAVORITE
COOKIE CONNOISSEURS.

CONTENTS

INTRODUCTION

I'm so glad you're here! I'm guessing you love cookies as much as I do...am I right? Cookies are probably my favorite things to bake. They can be quick and easy, assembled between naps, or more complicated and intricate like macarons (which become addictive to make, I promise!). I always reach to baking when I'm happy and I have something to celebrate or when I'm stressed and need some time to think and chill out. Something about the smell of creamed butter and sugar or just-baked cookies wafting in the air makes everything seem right.

To back up, I am a self-taught baker, raised in a family where nobody feels the slightest inclination to edit themselves. They'll say whether they like or don't like something, which forced me to try and make the best sweet treats from the very start. I have spent time as a caterer, which taught me about scaling recipes, the advantages of preparation and the necessity of time management. I also worked at a bakery, which taught me the importance of consistency that only a well-crafted recipe can produce. All of this is great news for you.

In 2014 I started the blog DisplacedHousewife with the goal of spreading some joy while sharing some of my favorite recipes. My time writing for the blog has probably had the biggest impact on how I write recipes. I strive for clarity and detail so that it's as if I'm there with you every step of the way, making sure your sweets turn out as perfect as possible.

When I started DisplacedHousewife, I dabbled between sharing sweet and savory recipes, looking for some rhythm between myself and my readers that made sense with my tastes and cravings. After two years of posting recipes weekly and getting to know my audience, I realized two things: I truly adore baking and my followers got really excited when I published cookie recipes.

That's why I was so excited to create this collection of cookies just for this book. All of these recipes, save for a few, have never been published before. They're a collection of family favorites, inspiration from friends and family and the result of an overactive imagination that might have an unhealthy obsession with making the ultimate cookie.

My goal with every recipe is that it's easy to follow, delicious to taste and has something in there that makes you smile. I hope you'll cozy up to it, get a bit of a laugh and make some really delicious cookies. I want you to abuse it as a well-loved book needs to be abused: smeared with chocolate, coated in flour, corners turned down.

As a parent to two beautiful and completely bonkers kids—hi Stella and Gavin!—I am often just trying to squeeze in satisfying a colossal craving after work or before school or in between practices. I'm thinking most of you are also living this crazy, harried life? For that reason, I've included lots of tips, substitutions and make-ahead options, because DAMN we're busy and I want to help you satisfy your cravings as quickly and painlessly as possible. And more importantly, these cookies are accessible. They are often made with ingredients we have in our cupboards and the basics (usually) don't require too much skill. Even if you consider yourself a novice baker, you can nail a cookie. And if you have doubts, keep reading!

You're holding this book in your hot little hands because you want to up your cookie game, right? Maybe you want to dabble in the basics (Hella Chocolate Chip Cookies [page 10]), or maybe you're looking for a way to nail the next bake sale (Dazzling Drop Cookies [page 80]). Maybe you'd really like to stick the landing at your company potluck (Jazz Hands [page 50])? Or, and this is my favorite reason, you just want to sit in your pajamas on the couch, binge watch some television and eat some warm and delicious cookies (Cozy Classics [page 30]).

No matter the reason, the premise of the book is gourmet cookies, so whether it's a simpler cookie that can be mixed and baked in under an hour or something a little more complex, the goal is to dazzle. Are you feeling dazzling yet? Shall we dazzle together?

COOKIE SUCCESS

Before we get started, let's talk about some of my general cookie tips. I'll repeat them throughout the book, because I think they guarantee cookie success, but these are our basics:

1. Read through a new recipe before starting to make sure you have all of the ingredients, equipment and the time needed to get it done. I can't overstate the importance of this enough (and I'm the queen of ignoring this cardinal rule and paying the price, so don't do it!).

2. Never overmix your dough unless I tell you to really mix your dough. Most cookie dough needs a gentle hand. To that end, I often recommend mixing until the dough is just barely combined and the last bits of flour have disappeared into the dough.

3. Chill your dough. Sometimes I have you put the whole lump of dough in the fridge to firm up a bit. The longer it stays in the fridge, the puffier and tastier your cookies will get. Sometimes I have you put the dough in the freezer for a spell prior to baking. This helps the cookies keep their shape while baking. If you have a small freezer, consider putting them on plates. If I recommend these steps, don't skip them. The cookies will benefit from this cooling off time. Conversely, there are a handful of cookies that don't benefit from any fridge time, or can only tolerate a smidge.

4. Don't swap out ingredients unless I give you options. If a recipe calls for bread flour, use the bread flour. Can we talk bread flour? It gives your cookie some structure and chew. You'll love it. I promise. If you don't already have some, go get it. And don't swap another flour in its place. We'll have more bread flour talk later...but you won't get the same results if you change the receipe. End of story.

5. But do swap...add-ins! If I tell you to add dark chocolate chips to your cookie dough and you love milk chocolate, by all means add the milk chocolate. If I tell you to add dried cherries to a cookie but you only have dried cranberries and you don't want to run to the store, put the damn cranberries in. I don't want you changing out of your pajamas unless you have to.

6. I often get asked how I get a consistent look with my cookies because, let's be honest, buttery dough in a hot oven tends to do what it wants. But there are some things you can do to coax it into submission. As a general rule, I prefer to use my hands to roll dough balls rather than use cookie scoops. I prefer the way the resulting cookie looks. And yes, there is a difference in appearance. After making hundreds of dozens of cookies, I say this with 100 percent confidence. That said, some cookies, as noted throughout the book, were easier to make with a cookie scoop or with two spoons (this is usually the case with a damp dough), and I noted as such in those instances. However, I know that people are PASSSIONATE about their cookie scoops. And if that's you—great! Knock your socks off. If you don't (that's fine too!), just measure out one cookie and then eyeball the rest based on the one measured cookie. Another key tip to follow: when the cookies first come out of the oven use the edge of a spatula to nudge any lumps and bumps back into place. This last note is perhaps my favorite in turning out a nice, spherical cookie.

OK, more tips and suggestions to come. I hope you discover new ways to make some of your favorites and your taste buds are awakened by new spices and flavors. I'm really glad you're here. Let's bake some cookies, shall we?

HELLA **CHOCOLATE CHIP COOKIES**

I am 100 percent confident that I will never run out of ways to make chocolate chip cookies. They are, seriously, the most inspiring cookie out there. And anyone that says otherwise is a heretic and not to be trusted. In this chapter I played with fats and flours and add-ins to pull out different textures and flavors. There is literally a chocolate chip cookie here to fit every mood, occasion or whim.

Some tips to get you started:

- I prefer chopped chocolate to chips as they melt and form gorgeous pools of chocolate in your cookie. Does life get any better?

- As for chocolate, I almost always list dark chocolate in the ingredient list. However, if your taste skews towards milk chocolate or white chocolate, by all means reach for those. If you're feeling frisky, grab your favorite candy bar, chop it up and replace all or some of the chocolate in your cookie. You're most welcome.

- To get the prettiest cookie, place the side of the dough ball with the most chocolate chunks facing upright.

- As long as we're talking about looks, for almost all of the cookies in this book I would use a scoop to measure the correct size, and then gently roll the dough into a ball, place on the baking sheet and proceed with the instructions.

- Wrapped tightly, these cookie doughs can be stored in the fridge for up to 5 days, baking off cookies as you'd like to eat them. Additionally, the dough balls can be frozen in an airtight container for up to 2 months.

- When choosing add-ins, look to dried fruit, nuts and your candy aisle. When choosing caramels go for the soft ones. You'll chip a tooth if you go for a harder caramel. Oh, and don't forget puffed grains: traditional puffed rice, but we also dabble in puffed quinoa.

MY CLASSIC SOFT AND CHEWY
CHOCOLATE CHIP COOKIE

This is probably my most reached-for chocolate chip cookie recipe. It's all basic ingredients and requires no special technique other than letting the dough rest a bit in the fridge anywhere from 1 hour and up to several days. The longer your dough stays in the fridge, the more the brown sugar and vanilla notes of the cookie will intensify, and they will bake up puffier than if you just made the dough. None of these are bad things. The texture is soft and chewy (like the name implies) and melt-in-your-mouth delicious.

MAKES 30 COOKIES

8 tablespoons (115 g) unsalted butter, room temperature

1 cup (210 g) light brown sugar, packed

½ cup (96 g) granulated sugar

2 large eggs, room temperature

⅔ cup (158 ml) sunflower seed oil or other neutral oil

1 tablespoon (15 ml) milk, room temperature

1 tablespoon (15 ml) real vanilla extract

1½ cups (204 g) all-purpose flour

1½ cups (204 g) bread flour

1 teaspoon baking powder

1 teaspoon baking soda

1 teaspoon sea salt

2½ cups (300 g) dark chocolate, chopped

Sea salt flakes for dusting on top, optional

In an electric stand mixer fitted with the paddle attachment, add the butter, brown sugar and granulated sugar and mix on medium for 4 minutes, or until light and well blended. With the mixer on low, add in the eggs, one at a time, completely mixing the first before adding the second. Take care to scrape down the sides and bottom of the bowl so that everything is incorporated. Add the oil, milk and vanilla and mix for 1 minute more.

In another medium bowl, whisk together the all-purpose flour, bread flour, baking powder, baking soda and sea salt. Add this to the butter mixture and mix on low until barely combined and you still see streaks of flour. Add in the chocolate chunks and continue to mix on low until combined and the chocolate is evenly distributed throughout. Wrap tightly and set in the fridge for at least 1 hour for the dough to set up a bit.

When you're ready to bake, preheat your oven to 350°F (177°C). Make sure you have a rack in the top third of the oven at least 6 inches (15 cm) from the heat source and cover your baking sheets with parchment paper.

Gently roll 2 tablespoons (28 g) of dough into a ball. Place the dough balls on the covered baking sheet about 2 inches (5 cm) apart. If using the sea salt flakes, sprinkle a pinch on each dough ball.

Bake one sheet at a time in the top third of the oven for 11 minutes. Let cool on the baking sheets for 15 minutes, and then transfer the cookies to a rack to finish cooling.

FAVORITE THIN AND CRISPY

These cookies are crispy and thin, but they still contain enough chew that they won't shatter a tooth. I can't bear a cookie that's too crisp. I use European butter for these, which has more fat than American butter and a richer, tangier taste. It sounds a bit high maintenance to ask you to get European butter, but it's worth it. Trust me. These require zero fridge or freezer time, which makes them the perfect cookie to turn to when you want to satisfy a craving fast. So, pack your fridge with euro buttah.

MAKES 30 COOKIES

16 tablespoons (230 g) salted European butter, room temperature

1½ cups (288 g) granulated sugar

½ cup (105 g) light brown sugar, packed

2 large eggs, room temperature

1 tablespoon (15 ml) real vanilla extract

2½ cups (340 g) all-purpose flour

½ cup (68 g) bread flour

1 teaspoon baking powder

1 teaspoon baking soda

½ teaspoon sea salt

2½ cups (300 g) dark chocolate, coarsely chopped

Preheat your oven to 350°F (177°C) and cover several baking sheets with parchment paper.

In an electric stand mixer fitted with the paddle attachment, add the butter, granulated sugar and brown sugar and beat on medium for about 4 minutes, or until pale and fluffy. Add the eggs, one at a time, making sure the first is fully blended before adding in the next. Be sure to scrape down the sides and bottom of the bowl so that everything is incorporated. Add in the vanilla and mix for 1 minute more. Remove the bowl from mixer and set aside.

In a medium bowl, whisk together the all-purpose flour, bread flour, baking powder, baking soda and sea salt. Add this to the butter mixture and stir until barely blended and you still see streaks of flour. Add in the chocolate chunks and continue to blend until the chocolate is evenly distributed throughout.

Roll 2 tablespoons (28 g) of dough into balls and press down slightly to form a disc. Place the dough balls on the covered baking sheet about 2 inches (5 cm) apart.

Bake one sheet at a time for 11 to 13 minutes in the center of the oven. Bang the baking sheet on the counter several times after removing from the oven to collapse the cookies a bit...This will make the finished cookies even crispier. Cool on the baking sheet for 10 to 15 minutes, and then move the cookies to a rack to finish cooling.

BROWN BUTTER CHOCOLATE CHIP COOKIES

If I ruled the world, it would be filled with more brown butter. And it would be absolutely mandatory in a chocolate chip cookie. Browning the butter really brings out those delicious caramel flavors that are naturally present in a really good chocolate chip cookie. This cookie is, wait for it, soft. Chewy. And utterly delicious.

MAKES 30 COOKIES

10 tablespoons (143 g) unsalted butter

1 cup (210 g) light brown sugar, packed

½ cup (96 g) granulated sugar

½ cup (118 ml) sunflower seed oil or other neutral oil

2 large eggs, room temperature

2 tablespoons (30 ml) milk, room temperature

3 teaspoons (15 ml) real vanilla extract

2¼ cups (306 g) all-purpose flour

¾ cup (103 g) bread flour

1 teaspoon baking powder

½ teaspoon baking soda

1 teaspoon sea salt

2½ cups (300 g) dark chocolate, chopped

Sea salt flakes for dusting on top, optional

Preheat your oven to 375°F (190°C). Place a rack in the top third of the oven at least 6 inches (15 cm) from the heat source and cover your baking sheets with parchment paper.

Put butter in a small saucepan and melt over medium heat. Once melted, crank up the heat to medium high. Continue stirring and look for small golden bits that will start to settle on the bottom of the pan. It will smell deliciously nutty and caramel-y. This should take around 3 to 5 minutes. Once this happens, take it off the heat and pour into a medium, heat-safe bowl to cool a bit.

When cooled slightly, whisk in the brown sugar, granulated sugar and oil. Once smooth, add in the eggs one at a time, completely mixing in the first before adding the second. Whisk in the milk and vanilla until blended. Be sure to scrape down the sides and bottom of the bowl to make sure everything is incorporated.

In a medium bowl, whisk together the all-purpose flour, bread flour, baking powder, baking soda and sea salt. Add the flour mixture to the brown butter mixture and mix until just blended and you still see streaks of flour. Add in the chocolate chunks and continue to blend until the chocolate is evenly distributed throughout.

Gently roll 2 tablespoons (28 g) of dough into a ball. Place the dough balls on the prepared baking sheet about 2 inches (5 cm) apart. Sprinkle each with a pinch of sea salt flakes, if using.

Bake one sheet at a time for 11 minutes in the top third of the oven. Let cool for 5 to 10 minutes on the baking sheet, and then transfer the cookies to a rack.

BIG-ASS OLIVE OIL CHOCOLATE CHIP COOKIES

The olive oil affects both the flavor and texture in this cookie. It first lends a fruitiness to the cookie and changes the flavor a bit from the classic but makes it delicious in surprising ways. From a texture perspective we get thin, crispy edges with a heavenly chewy center. If you haven't made cookies with olive oil before, the time has come.

MAKES 18 TO 20 HUGE COOKIES

1½ cups (330 g) light brown sugar, packed

⅔ cup (158 ml) good quality olive oil

½ cup (96 g) granulated sugar

6 tablespoons (86 g) unsalted butter, room temperature

2 large eggs, room temperature

1½ teaspoons (7 ml) pure vanilla extract

2 cups (272 g) all-purpose flour

1 cup (136 g) bread flour

1 teaspoon baking powder

1 teaspoon baking soda

1 teaspoon sea salt

2½ cups (330 g) dark chocolate, coarsely chopped or chips

Sea salt flakes for the tops, optional

Preheat your oven to 350°F (177°C) and line several baking sheets with parchment paper.

In an electric stand mixer fitted with the paddle attachment, mix your brown sugar, olive oil, granulated sugar and butter on medium for 2 minutes, or until smooth and fully incorporated. With the mixer on low, add in the eggs, one at a time, blending the first completely before adding in the second. Then add the vanilla and continue mixing until everything is well blended. Take the bowl out of the mixer and set aside.

In a medium bowl, whisk together the all-purpose flour, bread flour, baking powder, baking soda and sea salt. Add this to the wet ingredients and fold until the cookie dough is almost blended. You still want to see streaks of flour. Add the chocolate chunks and mix until evenly distributed throughout. Gently roll into 3-tablespoon-sized (42-g) balls, place on the prepared baking sheet and allow about 3½ inches (9 cm) of space between the dough balls to allow for spread. Sprinkle each with a pinch of sea salt flakes, if using.

Bake one sheet at a time in the center of the oven for about 12 to 14 minutes. They will look slightly underdone. Allow the cookies to cool on the baking sheet for 10 minutes, and then move to a rack to finish cooling.

> **TIP**
> Use a really delicious olive oil...one that you could drink straight from the bottle. It will lightly impart some flavor to the cookie.

EVERYTHING CHOCOLATE CHIP COOKIES

Lordy...let's talk about puffed quinoa. It adds the most amazing crispy surprise to things—I want to add it to everything. If you haven't had puffed quinoa before, I highly suggest you get some, stat. This cookie has it all...Brown butter? Check. Chewy? Yep. Slightly crispy edges? Yep, those too. These cookies are stuffed with toasted pecans, dark chocolate, puffed quinoa and dried tart cherries. Basically, all of my favorite things added to one cookie.

MAKES 30 COOKIES

10 tablespoons (143 g) unsalted butter

1⅓ cups (293 g) light or dark brown sugar, packed

⅓ cup (67 g) granulated sugar

½ cup (118 ml) sunflower seed oil or other neutral oil

2 large eggs, room temperature

1 tablespoon (15 ml) real vanilla extract

2 cups (272 g) all-purpose flour

1 cup (136 g) bread flour

1 teaspoon baking powder

1 teaspoon baking soda

1 teaspoon sea salt

2 cups (240 g) dark chocolate, coarsely chopped

1 cup (60 g) puffed quinoa

1 cup (140 g) dried tart cherries

¾ cup (91 g) pecans, toasted and coarsely chopped

Sea salt flakes for dusting on top, optional

Preheat your oven to 350°F (177°C). Place a rack in the top third of the oven at least 6 inches (15 cm) from the heat source and cover your baking sheets with parchment paper.

Put the butter in a medium saucepan and melt over medium heat. Once melted, crank up the heat to medium high. Continue stirring and look for small golden bits that will start to settle on the bottom of the pan. It will smell deliciously nutty and caramel-y. This should take around 3 to 5 minutes. Once this happens, take it off the heat and pour into a large, heat-safe bowl to cool a bit.

When cooled slightly, whisk in the brown sugar, granulated sugar and oil. Once smooth, add in the eggs one at a time, completely mixing in the first before adding the second. Whisk in the vanilla until blended. Be sure to scrape down the sides and bottom of the bowl to make sure everything is incorporated.

In another medium bowl, whisk together the all-purpose flour, bread flour, baking powder, baking soda and sea salt. Add this to the brown butter mixture and mix until just combined and you still see streaks of flour. Add in the chocolate chunks, quinoa, cherries and pecans and continue to blend until just combined. This dough is loaded with goodies and some may have a hard time adhering to the dough. Just force them back in there.

Gently roll 2 tablespoons (28 g) of dough into a ball. Place the dough balls on the covered baking sheet about 2 inches (5 cm) apart and press down slightly to form discs. Sprinkle each with a pinch of sea salt flakes, if using.

Bake one sheet at a time for 11 minutes in the top third of the oven. Let the cookies cool for 10 minutes on the baking sheet, and then transfer to a rack to finish cooling.

TIP

Puffed quinoa is basically just quinoa that has been cooked over high heat until it puffs up (like popcorn, but not even remotely as dramatic). You can buy it ready-made or make it yourself in a screaming hot Dutch oven.

TAHINI CHOCOLATE MACADAMIA NUT COOKIES

This is a classic chocolate chip cookie that gets its crunchy texture and a nutty, slightly smoky flavor from the tahini. I think it's perfect with chocolate and macadamia nuts...but you could add in cherries for a sweet contrast or puffed quinoa for additional texture. Be sure to use pure tahini with no other flavorings in it.

MAKES 36 COOKIES

1½ cups (330 g) light brown sugar, packed

8 tablespoons (115 g) unsalted butter, room temperature

½ cup (96 g) granulated sugar

2 large eggs, room temperature

1 large egg yolk, room temperature

½ cup (71 g) tahini, well stirred and room temperature

½ cup (118 ml) sunflower seed oil or other neutral oil

3 teaspoons (15 ml) pure vanilla extract

2 cups (272 g) all-purpose flour

¾ cup (103 g) bread flour

1½ teaspoons (6 g) baking soda

1 teaspoon sea salt

2½ cups (300 g) dark chocolate, coarsely chopped or chips

1 cup (120 g) macadamia nuts, coarsely chopped

In an electric stand mixer fitted with the paddle attachment, mix your brown sugar, butter and granulated sugar on medium for 4 minutes, or until light and fluffy. With the mixer on low, add in the eggs and egg yolk one at a time, making sure each is well blended before adding in the next. Add in the tahini, oil and vanilla and mix on low until everything is well blended. Be sure to scrape down the sides and bottom of the bowl.

In a medium bowl, whisk together the all-purpose flour, bread flour, baking soda and sea salt. Add the flour mixture to the electric stand mixer and mix on low until the cookie dough is barely blended. You still want to see streaks of flour. Take the bowl out of your stand mixer and fold in the chocolate and macadamia nuts until just mixed. Wrap tightly and refrigerate for 2 to 3 hours or more to firm up the dough. If using a cookie scoop or spoons, you can scoop the dough right away. It may yield a slightly flatter cookie without the fridge time.

Preheat your oven to 350°F (177°C). Make sure the rack is in the middle of your oven. Line your baking sheets with parchment paper.

Roll into balls of about 2 tablespoons (28 g) each and place on the prepared baking sheet. Allow about 2 inches (5 cm) of space between the dough balls.

Bake one sheet at a time in center of the oven for about 11 minutes. Allow the cookies to cool on the baking sheet for 5 minutes, and then move to a rack to finish cooling.

GF CHOCOLATE CHIP COOKIES

The biggest problem I've found with gluten-free cookies is texture. Letting the dough rest overnight allows the gluten-free flour time to absorb the liquid. I also added some milk into the dough for additional protein and added structure. We are a very pro-gluten family, but my kids love it when I make these.

MAKES 24 COOKIES

11 tablespoons (158 g) unsalted butter

1⅓ cups (293 g) dark or light brown sugar, packed

¼ cup (48 g) granulated sugar

½ cup (118 ml) sunflower seed oil or other neutral oil

2 large eggs, room temperature

2 tablespoons (30 ml) milk

3 teaspoons (15 ml) real vanilla extract

3 cups (408 g) gluten-free cup-for-cup flour

1 teaspoon baking powder

½ teaspoon baking soda

1 teaspoon sea salt

2½ cups (300 g) dark chocolate, chopped

Sea salt flakes for dusting on top, optional

Put the butter in a medium saucepan and melt over medium heat. Once melted, crank up the heat to medium high. Continue stirring and look for small golden bits that will start to settle on the bottom of the pan. It will smell deliciously nutty and caramel-y. This should take around 3 to 5 minutes. Once this happens, take it off the heat and pour into a medium, heat-safe bowl to cool a bit.

Once cooled slightly, whisk in the brown sugar, granulated sugar and oil. Once smooth, add in the eggs one at a time, completely mixing in the first before adding the second. Whisk in the milk and vanilla until blended. Be sure to scrape down the sides and bottom of the bowl to make sure everything is incorporated.

In another medium bowl, whisk together the gluten-free flour, baking powder, baking soda and sea salt. Add this to the brown butter mixture and mix completely. Add in the chocolate chunks and continue to blend until combined. Wrap tightly and stash in the fridge for 24 hours.

When ready to bake, preheat your oven to 350°F (177°C). Place a rack in the top third of the oven at least 6 inches (15 cm) from the heat source and cover your baking sheets with parchment paper.

Gently roll 2 tablespoons (28 g) of dough into a ball. Place the dough balls on the covered baking sheet about 2 inches (5 cm) apart. Press down to form each into a disc. Sprinkle each with a pinch of sea salt flakes, if using.

Bake one sheet at a time for 11 minutes in the top third of the oven. Let the cookies cool for 5 to 10 minutes on the baking sheet, and then transfer them to a rack.

> **TIP**
> My favorite gluten-free flour is Thomas Keller's Cup For Cup. Expensive, but worth it in my opinion. Whatever gluten-free flour you choose, make sure it is a cup-for-cup or measure-for-measure style.

BROWN BUTTER MUSCOVADO
CHOCOLATE CHUNK COOKIE BARS

This is basically a gooey brownie masquerading as a chocolate chip bar cookie. The muscovado and brown butter give this major caramel vibes, and it is just begging for a big scoop of ice cream. More than just a bar cookie...this deserves full dessert status. This has a nice crisp lid and edges, with a chewy, gooey center. You absolutely HAVE TO let these cool completely before cutting if you want a clean cut. Non-negotiable.

MAKES 15 COOKIES

8 tablespoons (115 g) unsalted butter

1 cup (210 g) dark muscovado sugar, packed

½ cup (96 g) granulated sugar

⅓ cup (79 ml) sunflower seed oil or other neutral oil

2 large eggs, room temperature

1 egg yolk, room temperature

2 tablespoons (30 ml) milk, room temperature

1 tablespoon (15 ml) real vanilla extract

1½ cups (204 g) bread flour

1½ cups (204 g) all-purpose flour

1 teaspoon baking powder

1 teaspoon baking soda

1 teaspoon sea salt

1½ cups (180 g) dark chocolate, chopped

Sea salt flakes for dusting on top, optional

Preheat your oven to 375°F (190°C). Grease an 8 x 11–inch (20 x 28–cm) casserole dish and line with parchment paper, letting the excess fall over the sides.

Put the butter in a medium saucepan and melt over medium heat. Once melted, crank up the heat to medium high. Continue stirring and look for small golden bits that will start to settle on the bottom of the pan. It will smell deliciously nutty and caramel-y. This should take around 3 to 5 minutes. Once this happens, take it off the heat and pour into a medium, heat-safe bowl to cool a bit.

When cooled slightly, whisk in the muscovado, granulated sugar, oil, eggs, egg yolk, milk and vanilla until thoroughly blended.

In another medium bowl, whisk together the bread flour, all-purpose flour, baking powder, baking soda and sea salt. Add this to the butter mixture and stir until barely blended. Add in the chocolate chunks and continue to blend until just combined and the chocolate is evenly distributed.

Pour the mixture into the prepared baking dish. Dampen your hands and gently press down so that it covers the bottom of the dish. Bake in the center of the oven for 25 minutes. It will continue to cook and firm up as it cools. Sprinkle with sea salt flakes, if desired. Let cool completely before cutting. These are great the same day as they're made and equally dazzling the next.

TIP

If you use a larger or smaller pan be sure to adjust your bake time accordingly. Additionally, these were tested in ceramic pans. Note, if you use a metal pan check earlier for doneness as it could affect the bake time.

STUFFED PRETZEL CARAMEL SKILLET COOKIE

I'm gonna blow the lid off of skillet cookies: You can basically make most any drop cookie into a skillet cookie. You'll need to increase the bake time, and I throw in some added ingredients to try and keep things light and cheerful, but basically, it's a cookie recipe. For this one I got a little frisky with the add-ins: pretzels, caramel and hella chocolate...what's not to love?!

MAKES 30 COOKIES

8 tablespoons (115 g) unsalted butter

1¼ cups (275 g) light or dark brown sugar, packed

⅔ cup (158 ml) sunflower seed oil or other neutral oil

¼ cup (48 g) granulated sugar

2 large eggs, room temperature

1 large egg yolk, room temperature

2 tablespoons (30 ml) milk, room temperature

1 tablespoon (15 ml) real vanilla extract

1½ cups (204 g) all-purpose flour

1½ cups (204 g) bread flour

1 teaspoon baking powder

1 teaspoon baking soda

1 teaspoon sea salt

2 cups (240 g) dark chocolate, coarsely chopped

1 cup (40 g) chopped small pretzels, some broken, some whole

¾ cup (90 g) caramel candy, chopped

Preheat your oven to 350°F (177°C). Butter a 10-inch (25-cm) cast-iron skillet and make sure you have a rack in the top third of the oven, at least 6 inches (15 cm) from the heat source.

Place the butter in a medium saucepan and melt over medium heat. Once melted, crank up the heat to medium high. Continue stirring and look for small golden bits that will start to settle on the bottom of the pan. It will smell deliciously nutty and caramel-y. This should take around 3 to 5 minutes. When this happens, take it off the heat and pour into a medium, heat-safe bowl to cool a bit. Once cool, stir in the brown sugar, oil, granulated sugar, eggs, egg yolk, milk and vanilla and mix until blended. Set aside.

In another medium bowl, whisk together the all-purpose flour, bread flour, baking powder, baking soda and sea salt. Add this to the butter mixture, stirring until barely combined and you still see streaks of flour. Add in the chopped chocolate, pretzels and caramel and stir until combined and everything is evenly distributed throughout. Add the dough to the skillet, patting it down to smooth any bumps and lumps.

Bake for 22 minutes in the top third of the oven. Wait at least 45 minutes to serve, and I strongly urge you to serve with vanilla ice cream.

TIPS

For the photo, I used three 6-inch (15-cm) petite cast-iron skillets, placed on a baking sheet to catch any overflow, and reduced the bake time to 15 to 17 minutes. Also, if you can't be bothered browning the butter, you can melt it. These would also be delicious with some sea salt dusted on top.

COZY
CLASSICS

ALSO KNOWN AS GATEWAY COOKIES

Classic cookies, the ones listed in this chapter, are and always have been my Achilles' heel. The simplicity of their ingredients means that they can often be made on a moment's notice with whatever you happen to have in your cupboards or fridge. Translation: a cookie binge is usually possible in less than an hour's time.

They're the cookies we smelled as kids, the ones we first learned to make as teenagers and the ones we may have burned in college when we learned that combining baking and drinking presents certain challenges. I seem to relearn this every five years or so.

That's why I call this collection of cookies "gateway" cookies. Once you get your toes wet making these you'll thirst for more. And while these are classic cookies with their jazz hands not overtly waving in your face, they are classics for a reason. I like to think that the combination of spices and technique that I share with you for my favorite classic cookies will reinvigorate these gems for you.

I pulled chocolate chip cookies into their own chapter because they are a cookie that I never tire of futzing with...so check out Hella Chocolate Chip Cookies (page 10) for all of the iterations.

Before you get started with the Cozy Classics, here are some ways to enjoy your cookies long after you've made your dough:

- All of these cookie doughs, minus the meringue, can handle some time in the fridge, and some need it. You can wrap them up tightly and forget about them for a day or two...up to 5 days...baking off cookies as the cravings hit. Just note that the longer your dough sits in the fridge, the puffier the cookie will be.

- All of these cookies, minus the meringue and the madeleines, can be rolled into balls, placed on a baking sheet in a single layer and frozen solid. Once frozen, place in an airtight container. The dough balls will be good for up to 2 months.

Let's get cozy, shall we?

A SUGAR COOKIE FOR EVERY OCCASION

I wanted to create a great sugar cookie that didn't just make pretty cut-out cookies, but also actually tasted delicious. I'm not a fan of a sugar cookie that is shatteringly crispy or that gets so puffy you lose the detail of your favorite cookie cutter. This cookie is perfectly chewy, slightly crispy around the edges and holds its shape well when it gets a brief spell in the freezer prior to baking. These are great decorated for a holiday using the glaze or simply served with a smear of buttercream and some festive sprinkles.

MAKES 48 COOKIES

24 tablespoons (344 g) unsalted butter, cut into 24 pieces, room temperature

1¼ cups (240 g) granulated sugar

¼ cup (55 g) light brown sugar, packed

2 large eggs, room temperature

2 teaspoons (11 ml) real vanilla extract

3½ cups (420 g) all-purpose flour, plus more for rolling the cookies

1 cup (136 g) bread flour

1 teaspoon sea salt

½ teaspoon baking powder

½ teaspoon baking soda

To make the cookies, in an electric stand mixer fitted with the paddle attachment, add the butter, granulated sugar and brown sugar and mix on medium until light and fluffy, about 4 minutes. Scrape down the sides and bottom of the bowl and add in the eggs, one at a time, making sure to completely blend the first before adding the second. Add in the vanilla and blend for 1 minute more, again scraping down the sides and bottom of the bowl.

In a large bowl, whisk together the flour, bread flour, sea salt, baking powder and baking soda. Add this to the butter mixture and run the machine for 1 minute more, or until blended. Separate into two equal halves and pat each mound of dough into a disc. Wrap tightly in plastic wrap and stash in the fridge for 15 minutes to rest.

Preheat the oven to 375°F (190°C) and cover several baking sheets with parchment paper.

Let the dough sit for 10 minutes or longer to soften. Place the dough between two lightly floured layers of parchment. If you have a silicone baking mat, place it underneath the parchment to keep it from sliding on the counter. You'll know the dough is soft enough to roll when it doesn't crack and resist being rolled out. Roll the dough to ¼- to ½-inch (0.5- to 1.3-cm) thickness. If I'm using a round cutter, I go for thicker cookies. If I'm using detailed cookie cutters, I will roll the dough on the thinner side. When rolling the dough, it is important to roll the dough and then give it a quarter turn and roll again. Repeat until you get the desired thickness, adding more flour as you go to keep the dough from sticking.

Sprinkle a small bit of flour over the top of the dough and dip your cookie cutter (I use a 2-inch [5-cm] round cutter) in flour. Press as many shapes as possible on the dough. Place the cookies on the parchment covered baking sheet, leaving 1 inch (2.5 cm) between cookies—they won't spread much. Repeat with the other disc of dough, re-rolling dough and cutting cookies until the dough is gone. Ideally only re-roll the dough once; any more than that could yield a tough cookie.

(continued)

GLAZE

2 cups (260 g) powdered sugar

4 tablespoons (60 ml) milk, or more to thin

Gel food coloring, optional

1 to 2 teaspoons (5 to 10 ml) extract, fresh fruit zest or fresh fruit juice to flavor, optional

Sprinkles, optional

EASY BUTTERCREAM FOR ANY OCCASION

8 tablespoons (115 g) unsalted butter, cut into 8 pieces, room temperature

2½ cups (325 g) powdered sugar

1 to 2 tablespoons (15 to 30 ml) milk

1 to 2 teaspoons extract, fresh fruit zest or fresh fruit juice to flavor, optional

Gel food coloring, optional

Sprinkles, optional

Place the cookies in the freezer for 15 to 20 minutes and then take them directly from the freezer to the middle rack of the oven and bake one sheet at a time for 8 to 9 minutes. It's crucial not to overbake these. Let the cookies cool for 5 minutes on the baking sheet, and then transfer them to a rack to finish cooling.

To make the glaze, in a medium bowl whisk the powdered sugar, milk, food coloring and extract, if using, until smooth. Either drizzle the glaze over the cookies or dip the tops of each cookie in the glaze, letting the excess fall back into the bowl. Proceed with sprinkles or whatever your heart desires.

To make the buttercream, in an electric stand mixer fitted with the paddle, add the butter, powdered sugar and milk and mix on medium until smooth. Add in any extracts for flavor (simple lemon zest and juice is delicious) or food coloring, if using. Add more powdered sugar in 1 tablespoon (8 g) increments if the buttercream is too thin, or conversely add more milk in 1 teaspoon increments if the buttercream is too thick. Proceed with sprinkles, if using.

FRESH LEMON MADELEINES

When we lived in Beijing we would go to Maison Boulud for cocktails and fresh-made madeleines. My only regret is that the restaurant didn't open sooner in my China tenure so this could have been a weekly occurrence. These madeleines burst with bright lemon flavors and teeter that classic madeleine line between cake and cookie. Madeleines are always best eaten the day they are made, which works perfectly with a batter that can sit in the fridge for several days and still perform like a champ.

MAKES 24 MADELEINES

8 tablespoons (115 g) unsalted butter, really softened and cut into 8 pieces

2 large eggs, room temperature

⅔ cup (128 g) granulated sugar

1 tablespoon (15 ml) whole milk, room temperature

1 tablespoon (9 g) lemon zest

1 teaspoon vanilla bean paste or real vanilla extract

⅔ cup plus 1 tablespoon (101 g) all-purpose flour

1 tablespoon (9 g) cornstarch

½ teaspoon baking powder

½ teaspoon sea salt

To make the cookies, grease two 3¼ x 1½–inch (8.3 x 3.7–cm) nonstick madeleine tins and place in the freezer for at least 30 minutes. If your room temperature butter isn't soft enough to easily smear on a plate, then give it 10 seconds on high in the microwave to give it the correct consistency. Set aside.

In an electric mixer fitted with the whisk attachment, whisk the eggs and sugar on high for about 5 minutes, or until pale yellow and thick like mayonnaise. Add in the milk, lemon zest and vanilla and run the machine on low for 1 minute more.

In a small bowl, whisk together the flour, cornstarch, baking powder and salt. Add the flour mixture and softened butter to the egg mixture and run the mixer on low for about 40 seconds. The mixture will be smooth and creamy with some small butter bits visible. Cover tightly with plastic wrap and store in the fridge for at least several hours or ideally overnight.

Preheat your oven to 375°F (190°C).

Add a heaping tablespoon (14 g) of batter to each madeleine well. Place the batter in the deep end of each well, not the middle. Do not smooth or flatten.

Bake one tin at a time in the center rack of the oven for 10 minutes. When done, the madeleines will be golden around the edges and puffed up in the middle. Let the cookies cool in the tin for 10 minutes before turning out onto a rack. Place some parchment underneath the cooling rack.

(continued)

FRESH LEMON MADELEINES (CONTINUED)

FRESH LEMON GLAZE

1¼ cups (163 g) powdered sugar

3 to 4 tablespoons (45 to 60 ml) milk, or more to thin

1 tablespoon (9 g) lemon zest

To make the glaze, in a small bowl, whisk together the powdered sugar, milk and lemon zest. Add more milk, in 1-teaspoon increments, to thin to the desired consistency. You want the glaze to lightly coat the entire cookie. Dip each madeleine in the glaze, letting the excess glaze fall back into the bowl, and then place the cookie back on the rack for the glaze to set.

TIP

This is a great recipe to swap in other citrus in place of the lemon. Think blood orange, Cara Cara orange, Meyer lemon or key lime.

MADELEINE MAKING TIPS

I file madeleines under the same folder as I do macarons and meringues (and I'm not talking things that start with 'M'). I'm talking technique. They're the kind of recipes that don't have a lot of ingredients, but it's the technique that makes them fail or succeed.

- Use a nonstick madeleine pan. Invest in some really good nonstick madeleine tins. I don't like to have you buy extra equipment, but you'll save yourself some heartache, as I've found even the most painstakingly perfectly-prepared pan can produce madeleines that stick.

- Since nonstick madeleine tins are darker in color than stainless-steel tins, they bake at a lower temperature. If using a stainless-steel tin that isn't nonstick, butter and flour the crap out of it and increase the oven to 400°F (204°C) and bake for several additional minutes.

- Chill your pan and batter and don't skip either step.

- Madeleine tins vary in size and depth. It's important that the batter is placed at the deepest part of the well and that you don't even it out or make it tidy. If your tin is slightly larger or smaller than 3¼ x 1½–inch (8.3 x 3.7–cm), adjust your batter per cookie and also adjust your bake time.

FRENCH MERINGUES

I love the simplicity of meringues, but for years I made them all wrong. I wasn't baking them nearly as long as they needed. It makes me incredibly nervous to leave anything other than a side of beef in the oven for a full 2 hours. (Wine helps to ease the anxiety in case you were wondering.) A perfect meringue will be dried through to its core so it gives a nice, shattering crunch when bitten. I went for pure, classic meringue here with just a touch of vanilla as a subtle back note. Feel free to add some jazz hands with extracts (with little or no oil in them) or gel coloring.

MAKES ABOUT 35 TO 40 (1-INCH [2.5-CM]) MERINGUES

3 large egg whites, room temperature

¼ teaspoon cream of tartar

¼ teaspoon sea salt

⅓ cup (64 g) granulated sugar

⅓ cup (43 g) powdered sugar

½ teaspoon real vanilla extract

Preheat your oven to 200°F (93°C) and cover several baking sheets with parchment paper. If using, prepare your pastry bag by placing a round pastry tip in the bottom and place in a large glass or vase to make it easier to fill. You could also use a clean plastic storage bag with the corner cut out or use a 1½-inch (3.7-cm) cookie scoop to make sweet little mounds.

In an electric stand mixer fitted with the whisk attachment, add the egg whites, cream of tartar and salt. Make sure the bowl and whisk are freshly cleaned and dried. Whisk on medium for several minutes until the eggs are frothy, and then slowly add in the granulated sugar. Turn the mixer on high and when the meringue is shiny and glossy and looks like marshmallow fluff (and the whisk is leaving tracks in it) add in the powdered sugar and vanilla. Turn the mixer back on high until you reach stiff peaks, which should be just 1 minute more. The meringue will look glossy and hold its shape when you invert the whisk. The tip of the inverted meringue will be just shy of 12 o'clock. It should also feel smooth when you rub some between your fingers.

Scoop the meringue into the prepared piping bag, if using (otherwise use two spoons) and pipe or dollop 1-inch (2.5-cm) circles on the prepared baking sheet, allowing 1 inch (2.5 cm) between meringues for heat and air flow.

Bake one sheet at a time in the center rack of the oven for 2 hours. Check after 1 hour to make sure the meringues aren't taking on any color. Turn off the oven and let the meringues sit in there until completely cool; it could take several hours.

TIPS
- Make sure everything that touches the egg whites has been thoroughly cleaned, dried and is free from any oils.
- Don't attempt on a humid day, or really make sure they dry out completely before taking them out of the oven.

SNICKERDOODLES

Do snickerdoodles give you the warm and fuzzies too? This is one of those cookies that my mom made a lot growing up. And when the craving hits for snickerdoodles, no other cookie will satisfy. This recipe is a dream and results in a classic tangy, delicious, pillowy snickerdoodle—you just need to allow the dough several hours in the fridge to chill out and firm up. I give you permission to take a nap during this time.

MAKES 24 COOKIES

1 cup (210 g) light brown sugar, packed

8 tablespoons (115 g) unsalted butter, room temperature

½ cup (96 g) granulated sugar

2 large eggs, room temperature

⅔ cup (158 ml) sunflower seed oil or other neutral oil

3 teaspoons (15 ml) real vanilla extract

1½ cups (204 g) bread flour

1¼ cups (170 g) all-purpose flour

2 teaspoons (6 g) cream of tartar

1 teaspoon baking soda

1 teaspoon sea salt

COOKIE COATING

⅓ cup (64 g) granulated sugar

1 teaspoon ground cinnamon

In an electric stand mixer fitted with the paddle attachment, add the brown sugar, butter and granulated sugar and mix on medium until light and fluffy, about 4 minutes. With the mixer on low, add in the eggs one at a time, taking care to fully blend the first before adding the second. Be sure to scrape the sides and bottom of the bowl to make sure everything is incorporated. Add in the oil and vanilla and mix 1 minute more. Take the bowl out of the mixer.

In a medium bowl, whisk together the bread flour, all-purpose flour, cream of tartar, baking soda and salt. Add this to the butter mixture and stir until the flour just disappears. Wrap tightly and put in the fridge for several hours, or until firm.

Preheat your oven to 375°F (190°C) and cover several baking sheets with parchment paper. Make sure a rack is in the top third of the oven at least 6 inches (15 cm) from the heat source. This is where you'll bake your cookies.

To make the cookie coating, in a small bowl, whisk together the granulated sugar and cinnamon.

Roll 1½ tablespoons (21 g) of dough into a nice ball. Give the dough ball a generous coating of the cinnamon mixture and set on the baking sheet, allowing 2 inches (5 cm) of space between dough balls.

Bake one sheet at a time, in the top third of the oven, for 11 to 12 minutes. Let the cookies cool on the baking sheet for 10 minutes and then transfer to a rack.

TIP

If you like an uber puffy snickerdoodle, place the dough balls in the freezer for 10 to 15 minutes prior to baking.

OATMEAL RAISIN COOKIES

Is there a bigger MVP in the comfort cookie category? I think not. This is the cookie to make when you've had a long day at work or you just generally think your co-workers are assholes. I'm sure they're perfectly fine people any other day, just not today. This cookie is chewy, soft, perfectly spiced and will feel like that cashmere blanket you've been wanting to buy. Yep. It's that comforting. Take a bath while the dough chills. You deserve it.

MAKES 26 COOKIES

8 tablespoons (115 g) unsalted butter, room temperature

1 cup (210 g) light brown sugar, packed

½ cup (96 g) granulated sugar

3 large eggs, room temperature

½ cup (118 ml) sunflower seed oil or other neutral oil

1 tablespoon (15 ml) real vanilla extract

1 cup (136 g) bread flour

1 cup (136 g) all-purpose flour

1¼ teaspoons (3 g) cinnamon

1 teaspoon baking powder

1 teaspoon baking soda

1 teaspoon sea salt

½ teaspoon nutmeg

3 cups (273 g) old-fashioned rolled oats

2½ cups (365 g) raisins (I like the dark ones)

Preheat your oven to 350°F (177°C) and cover several baking sheets with parchment paper.

In an electric stand mixer fitted with the paddle attachment, add the butter, brown sugar and granulated sugar and mix on medium for 4 minutes, or until nice and fluffy. Scrape down the sides and bottom of the bowl to make sure everything is incorporated. With the mixer on low add the eggs one at a time, completely mixing the first before adding the next, and then add in the oil and vanilla and mix for 1 minute more, or until well blended.

In a small bowl, whisk together the bread flour, all-purpose flour, cinnamon, baking powder, baking soda, sea salt and nutmeg. Dump the flour mixture into the butter mixture and mix until the cookie dough is almost blended. You'll still see streaks of flour. Add your oatmeal and raisins and run the machine for 1 minute more, or until the raisins and oatmeal are evenly distributed throughout the dough. This dough is messy, so if you don't have a cookie scoop, try using two spoons, or you may want to chill the dough in the fridge for 30 to 60 minutes to firm it up.

When ready to bake, roll 2-tablespoon-sized (28-g) balls and allow 2 inches (5 cm) of space between them. With damp hands, gently press the tops down to form discs.

Bake one sheet at a time in the center of the oven for 12 to 13 minutes. Allow the cookies to cool on the baking sheet for 15 minutes and then move to a cooling rack to finish cooling down.

TIP

This is a great recipe to experiment with brown butter as it adds amazing depth to the flavor. If you'd like to try it that way, use all 8 tablespoons (115 g) of butter and follow the browning butter instructions for the Brown Butter Muscovado Snickerdoodles (page 89). Also, consider replacing the raisins with dried cherries, use dried cranberries around the holidays or a combination of chocolate and nuts to mix things up a bit. Get frisky.

SPICED CHEWY MOLASSES

I'm a big fan of molasses and ginger if you can't tell. These cookies are packed with spices and chew and might ignite the desire to throw on your fisherman's sweater, light a fire and pretend it's winter year round. If you'd like to explore this flavor power couple more, go check out Molasses Ginger Crackles (page 93), Spiced Gingerbread Cookies Two Ways (page 125) and Burnt Sugar Ginger Cookies (page 59).

MAKES 24 COOKIES

1 cup (210 g) dark brown sugar, packed

8 tablespoons (115 g) unsalted butter, room temperature

⅓ cup (79 ml) unsulphured molasses

2 large eggs, room temperature

1 large egg yolk, room temperature

⅓ cup (79 ml) sunflower seed oil or other neutral oil

1 tablespoon (14 g) fresh ginger, finely grated

3 teaspoons (15 ml) real vanilla extract

2 cups (272 g) all-purpose flour

1 cup (136 g) bread flour

1 tablespoon (8 g) ground ginger

2½ teaspoons (12 g) baking soda

2 teaspoons (5 g) cinnamon

1 teaspoon cloves

1 teaspoon sea salt

¼ teaspoon allspice

COOKIE COATING

½ cup (96 g) granulated sugar or sparkling sugar

In an electric-stand mixer fitted with the paddle attachment, beat the brown sugar and butter on medium until completely blended and fluffy, about 4 minutes. Scrape the sides and bottom of the bowl to make sure everything is incorporated. Add in the molasses and mix for 1 minute. With the mixer on low add in the eggs and egg yolk one at a time, making sure each is well blended before adding in the next. Add in the oil, fresh ginger and vanilla and mix on low for several minutes more until thoroughly combined. Take the bowl out of the stand mixer.

In a medium bowl, whisk together the all-purpose flour, bread flour, ground ginger, baking soda, cinnamon, cloves, salt and allspice. Pour the flour mixture into the butter-molasses mixture and fold in the flour until just combined. Wrap tightly and place in the fridge for at least several hours, or up to several days. This dough is sticky, do not skip this step.

When ready to bake, preheat the oven to 350°F (177°C) and cover several baking sheets with parchment paper.

For the cookie coating, place the sugar in a shallow bowl.

Gently roll 2 tablespoons (28 g) of dough into a ball and then roll the ball in the sugar. Cover each dough ball completely and do not shake off the excess. Place on the baking sheet allowing about 2 inches (5 cm) between each dough ball. Press each dough ball down slightly to form a disc. Dampen your hands if the dough is sticky.

Bake one sheet at a time for 11 to 12 minutes on the center rack of the oven. You want to slightly underbake these. Allow the cookies to cool on the sheet for 5 to 10 minutes, then transfer to a cooling rack.

CHOCOLATE CRINKLES

Crinkles remind me so much of my childhood. When my mom made crinkles, we were totally psyched. It's a chocolate cookie that boasts mega chocolate flavor that is amplified with a hit of freshly brewed espresso or extra strong coffee. I like my crinkles to have lots of big fissures over the tops. The key is to roll them thickly in the granulated sugar and then in the powdered sugar, taking care not to shake any off. These are rich and fudge-like in the interior. Think of them as little chocolate clouds. I prefer to roll the dough using my hands, rather than using a cookie scoop, to get the perfect little sphere. Just prepare yourself, it's messy business.

MAKES 27 COOKIES

1¾ cups (210 g) dark chocolate, finely chopped

8 tablespoons (115 g) unsalted butter, room temperature

1 tablespoon (15 ml) freshly brewed espresso or strong coffee

¾ cup (144 g) granulated sugar

¼ cup (55 g) light brown sugar, packed

2 large eggs, room temperature

3 teaspoons (15 ml) real vanilla extract

1½ cups (204 g) bread flour

½ cup (43 g) unsweetened dark (Dutch process) cocoa powder

1 teaspoon baking powder

¾ teaspoon baking soda

1½ teaspoons (7 g) sea salt

COOKIE COATING

¾ cup (144 g) granulated sugar

¾ cup (98 g) powdered sugar

In a medium, heat-safe bowl, add the chocolate, butter and espresso and set over a medium saucepan of simmering water. Do not let the bowl touch the water or let the water come to a boil. Stir frequently until melted and smooth. Take off of the heat, add the granulated sugar and brown sugar and mix until smooth. Whisk in the eggs and vanilla. Set aside.

In a medium bowl, whisk together the bread flour, cocoa powder, baking powder, baking soda and sea salt. Add this to the chocolate mixture and blend in as few strokes as possible. Wrap tightly and refrigerate for 1 to 2 hours, or until the dough has firmed up.

Preheat your oven to 350°F (177°C) and cover several baking sheets with parchment paper.

To make the cookie coating, put the granulated sugar and powdered sugar in separate, shallow bowls to roll the cookie dough in. Roll 1½ tablespoons (21 g) of dough into a ball, plop it into the granulated sugar and cover completely. Don't shake any off as you want it well coated. Then roll the balls in the powdered sugar. Again, don't shake off the excess.

Place the covered dough balls on the baking sheet, about 2 inches (5 cm) apart from each other. Bake one sheet at a time in the center of the oven for 11 minutes. Don't overbake...they will be soft and appear underdone when you pull them out of the oven.

Let the cookies cool on the sheet for 15 minutes. Then remove the cookies and place on a cooling rack.

> **TIP**
> Around the holidays, add ½ teaspoon of peppermint extract when you add in the vanilla and, if you're really feeling festive, some chopped up peppermint bark.

SUPER PEANUT-Y PEANUT BUTTER COOKIES

I just lovvvvveeee a good peanut butter cookie. I wanted these loaded with peanut flavor, studded with salty, crunchy peanuts and with a texture that is soft, chewy and, dare I say, cloud-like. Peanuts in the form of peanut butter as well as handfuls of salted, roasted peanuts in the batter deliver in full force. Please don't go for raw peanuts, I beg of you. I love lots of raw nuts (yay cashews, yes hazelnuts), but raw peanuts are just sad compared to the flavor party that is salted and roasted peanuts.

MAKES 40 COOKIES

1½ cups (330 g) light brown sugar, packed

1¼ cups (317 g) smooth, natural peanut butter

8 tablespoons (115 g) unsalted butter, room temperature

½ cup (96 g) granulated sugar

2 large eggs, room temperature

⅓ cup (79 ml) sunflower seed oil or other neutral oil

3 teaspoons (15 ml) real vanilla extract

1½ cups (204 g) all-purpose flour

1¼ cups (170 g) bread flour

1 teaspoon baking powder

1 teaspoon baking soda

½ teaspoon sea salt

¾ cup (96 g) salted and roasted peanuts, chopped

Preheat your oven to 350°F (177°C). Cover several baking sheets with parchment paper.

In an electric stand mixer fitted with the paddle attachment, add the brown sugar, peanut butter, butter and granulated sugar and mix on medium for about 4 to 5 minutes, or until smooth. Add in the eggs one at a time, making sure the first is completely blended before adding the next, scraping down the sides and bottom of the bowl so that everything is incorporated. Add in the oil and vanilla and mix for 1 minute more.

In a medium-sized bowl whisk together the flour, bread flour, baking powder, baking soda and the sea salt. Pour the dry ingredients into the bowl with the butter-sugar mixture and mix on low until just blended. Add in the peanuts and mix for 1 minute more.

Roll the dough into balls, using about 1 tablespoon (14 g) of dough per ball, and gently press down to form little discs. Place on the prepared baking sheet, leaving 1½ inches (3.7 cm) between each dough disc. I like to press any cracks on the sides so that they're smooth. Use the tines of a fork to create marks on the cookie, dipping the fork in flour as necessary to prevent sticking.

Bake one sheet at a time for 9 minutes on the center rack of the oven. They will be very soft when you get them out of the oven. Let them cool for 5 to 10 minutes on the baking sheet before transferring to a cooling rack.

TIP
Add chocolate chips. Enough said.

JAZZ **HANDS**

Looking to impress your obnoxious co-worker or bossy in-law? Look no further, these are the cookies for when you really want to dazzle and have some extra time on your hands. I love making a classic chocolate chip cookie or a simple drop cookie when cookie cravings hit like a thunderbolt. But there are other times when I want to spend a bit more time in the kitchen and make something spectacular. For those such occasions, I bring out the jazz hands: the cookies that have an unexpected flavor or a new, fresh appearance or just make those that eat them feel like they're enjoying something extra special.

In this chapter we'll cover things like liquefying sugar and nestling fresh ginger in there to create a show-stopping, life changing, Burnt Sugar Ginger Cookie (page 59). I swear I'm not being dramatic...they're really good. We'll futz with pecan brittle and turn it into bark and then shove it into the most delicious Pecan Brittle Bark Cookie (page 60). We'll make thumbprints and macarons (yes, yes you can), truffles and meringues. We'll bake with booze, because sometimes life demands it.

One cookie to be sure and check out is the Five-Spice Cranberry Mooncake Cookies (page 74). When I lived in Beijing I became obsessed with mooncake molds. They're these gorgeous molds carved out of wood in all kinds of beautiful designs from Chinese characters to flowers. They're traditionally used during the Mid-Autumn Festival to make classic mooncakes (think lotus seed paste and cured duck eggs). For our mooncake cookies, I reach for a sturdy sugar cookie dough and stuff it with a cranberry and white chocolate mixture. The cranberries gently stain the exterior, highlighting the design from the mooncake molds. For these, we use a more readily available plastic mooncake mold that's a little easier to work with. And lastly, a light citrus glaze glosses up the tops. These cookies have mega jazz hands.

The Jazz Hands cookies are going to require maybe a few more steps, perhaps a unique ingredient or kitchen tool and maybe, just maybe, a wee bit more of your precious time. But I think they're worth it. So, before we begin, I'm going to need you to create your ideal baking vibe. Candles, music, a cocktail or tea, some cozy slippers, your favorite leisure wear?

Let's make something magical, shall we?

RED VELVET MADELEINES

There is something so striking about anything red velvet, making them the perfect recipe to have on hand for when you're feeling especially dramatic. Which is pretty often at our house. The cookie itself has a soft chocolate note (amplified by the chocolate extract) and then they're coated with the perfect bit of vanilla bean glaze. These are best made with a nonstick madeleine tin. I've found if you heavily butter and flour a regular madeleine tin, it makes the red velvet cookies less vibrant and kind of gunky, for lack of a better term, on their underbelly.

MAKES 24 MADELEINES

½ cup (115 g) unsalted butter, really softened and cut into 8 small pieces

2 large eggs, room temperature

⅔ cup (128 g) granulated sugar

2 teaspoons (10 ml) gel red food coloring (I used Americolor Super Red 120)

1 tablespoon (15 ml) whole milk, room temperature

1 teaspoon real vanilla extract

1 teaspoon chocolate extract

⅔ cup (90 g) all-purpose flour

1 tablespoon (7 g) unsweetened dark (Dutch process) cocoa powder

1 tablespoon (9 g) cornstarch

½ teaspoon baking powder

½ teaspoon sea salt

VANILLA BEAN GLAZE

1¼ cups (163 g) powdered sugar

3 to 4 tablespoons (45 to 60 ml) milk, or more to thin

½ vanilla bean, split and scraped

Grease two 3¼ x 1½–inch (8.3 x 3.7–cm) nonstick madeleine tins and place in the freezer for at least 30 minutes. If your room temperature butter isn't soft enough to easily smear on a plate, then give it 10 seconds on high in the microwave to give it the correct consistency. Set aside.

In an electric mixer fitted with the whisk attachment, whisk the eggs and sugar on high for about 5 minutes, or until pale yellow and thick like mayonnaise. Add in the food coloring, milk, vanilla and chocolate extract and continue to run the machine on low for 2 minutes more, or until the food coloring is evenly distributed throughout the batter.

In a small bowl, whisk together the flour, cocoa powder, cornstarch, baking powder and salt. Add the flour mixture and softened butter to the egg mixture and run the mixer on low for about 40 seconds. The mixture will be smooth and creamy with some small butter bits visible. Cover the dough tightly with plastic wrap and chill in the fridge for several hours or, ideally, overnight.

Preheat your oven to 375°F (190°C).

Add a heaping tablespoon (14 g) of batter to each madeleine well. Place the batter in the deep end of each well, not the middle. Do not smooth or flatten.

Bake one sheet at a time on the center rack of the oven for 10 minutes. When done the madeleines will be puffed up in the middle. Let the cookies cool in the tin for 10 minutes before turning out onto a rack. Place some parchment paper beneath the rack.

To make the glaze, in a small bowl, whisk together the powdered sugar, milk and vanilla. Add more milk, in 1 teaspoon increments, if the glaze seems too thick. Dip the madeleines in the glaze and place back on the rack until set. These are best when eaten the same day they are baked.

TIP
Refer to the madeleine tips on page 37.

CHOCOLATE STOUT COOKIES
WITH IRISH BUTTERCREAM

If you're anything like me, you love to bake thematically. The holidays? Obviously, there are spices and cranberries involved. Valentine's Day? Bring on the chocolate and raspberries. Come March? Give me any type of Irish booze and I'll see how many ways I can work it into a dessert. For this, we reach for a nice, thick stout beer. I usually grab a Guinness and then Bailey's because it really needs no defining. The chocolate flavor is really pulled back in the cookie, letting the stout shine through. And this buttercream. Don't even get me started. Come St. Patrick's Day, you're sorted.

MAKES 36 COOKIES

16 tablespoons (230 g) unsalted butter, room temperature

1 cup (210 g) light brown sugar, packed

1 cup (192 g) granulated sugar

2 large eggs, room temperature

2 tablespoons (30 ml) stout beer, room temperature

1 tablespoon (15 ml) real vanilla extract

1 cup (136 g) bread flour

1 cup (136 g) all-purpose flour

⅔ cup (56 g) unsweetened dark (Dutch process) cocoa powder

1½ teaspoons (6 g) baking powder

1 teaspoon baking soda

1 teaspoon sea salt

IRISH BUTTERCREAM

2½ cups (325 g) powdered sugar

8 tablespoons (115 g) unsalted butter, room temperature

3 tablespoons (44 ml) Irish cream liqueur

Preheat the oven to 350°F (177°C) and place a rack in the top third of the oven, at least 6 inches (15 cm) from the heat source. Cover several baking sheets with parchment paper.

In an electric stand mixer fitted with the paddle attachment, add the butter, brown sugar and granulated sugar and mix on medium for 4 minutes, or until light and fluffy. With the mixer on low, add the eggs one at a time, making sure one is well blended before adding the next. Add in the beer and vanilla and mix for 1 minute more.

In a medium bowl, whisk together the bread flour, all-purpose flour, cocoa powder, baking powder, baking soda and sea salt. Add to the butter mixture and mix on low until just combined. Make 1½-tablespoon (21-g) balls; this dough is sticky, so use a cookie scoop or two spoons. If the dough is too sticky to handle, chill in the fridge for 1 hour or so until firmed up. Leave 3 inches (7.7 cm) between the dough balls and place on the prepared baking sheet. Chill the balls in the freezer for 10 minutes or the refrigerator for 20 minutes.

Take the cookies from the freezer directly to the oven and bake one sheet at a time in the top third of the oven for 11 minutes. Let cool on the baking sheet for 5 minutes and then transfer to a rack to cool completely.

To make the buttercream, in an electric stand mixer fitted with the paddle attachment, mix the powdered sugar, butter and liqueur on medium for 4 minutes or until smooth. Smear some on the top of each cookie and serve.

COLD BREW COOKIES

I'm one of those people that only tries a trend once it's no longer new and trendy. I don't know what that's all about. But I didn't try cold brew until late last year and as a certified obsessed espresso drinker I was MINDBLOWN over how much I love it. So of course, I had to make a cookie out of it. The biggest distinction between cold brew and other coffees (drip, espresso, you name it) for me is how smooth it is. Nary a bitter bite in sight. These cookies are loaded with heaps of coffee flavor. So much so that I wouldn't eat one at 10 o'clock at night unless I wanted to stay up until dawn.

MAKES 32 COOKIES

1½ cups (330 g) light brown sugar, packed

8 tablespoons (115 g) unsalted butter, room temperature

½ cup (96 g) granulated sugar

2 large eggs, room temperature

1 egg yolk, room temperature

½ cup (118 ml) sunflower seed oil or other neutral oil

2 tablespoons (30 ml) cold brew concentrate

1 tablespoon (15 ml) real vanilla extract

1½ cups (204 g) all-purpose flour

1 cup (136 g) bread flour

⅔ cup (56 g) unsweetened dark (Dutch process) cocoa powder

1½ teaspoons (7 g) sea salt

1½ teaspoons (6 g) baking powder

1 teaspoon baking soda

1½ cups (180 g) white chocolate, coarsely chopped

1 cup (120 g) dark chocolate, coarsely chopped

1 cup (161 g) chocolate covered espresso beans, coarsely chopped

Preheat your oven to 350°F (177°C) and cover several baking sheets with parchment paper.

In an electric stand mixer fitted with the paddle attachment, add the brown sugar, butter and granulated sugar and mix on medium for 4 minutes or until light and fluffy. With the mixer on low add in the eggs and egg yolk one at a time, making sure the first is well blended before adding in the next. Make sure to scrape the sides and bottom of the bowl so that everything is incorporated. Add in the oil, cold brew and vanilla and run the machine for 1 minute more.

In a medium bowl, whisk together the all-purpose flour, bread flour, cocoa powder, salt, baking powder and baking soda. Add to the butter mixture, stirring until barely combined and you still see streaks of flour. Add in the white chocolate, dark chocolate and espresso beans, stirring until distributed evenly throughout the dough. Do not overmix. If the dough is sticky, place in the fridge for 20 to 30 minutes or until it's easier to handle.

Roll 2 tablespoons (28 g) of dough into a ball and set on the prepared baking sheet, leaving 2 inches (5 cm) of space between dough balls. Set the side that's studded with the most chocolate and espresso beans facing up for the prettiest cookie. Bake one sheet at a time on the center rack of the oven for 11 minutes. If they're a little too puffy when you get them out of the oven, bang the sheet on the counter once or twice to help them settle down. Let the cookies cool for 5 minutes on the baking sheet, and then transfer to a rack to finish cooling.

TIP

You can use fresh-brewed espresso or strong coffee in place of the cold brew.

BURNT SUGAR GINGER COOKIES

Ovenly has a recipe for burnt sugar which had me completely intrigued ever since I first laid eyes on it. I knew I wanted to mess around with it for a cookie, and I decided to create a super ginger-y cookie with it. But don't be overwhelmed with the amount of ginger in here. I promise, it's not too much. Unless, of course, you don't like ginger in which case you probably shouldn't be making this cookie. When making the burnt sugar, you aren't actually burning it, just stirring until it liquefies and turns a deep amber. I'm already thinking of a million more ways to use it!

MAKES 46 COOKIES

BURNT SUGAR GINGER

1 cup (192 g) granulated sugar

3 teaspoons (14 g) fresh ginger, finely grated

GINGER COOKIES

16 tablespoons (230 g) unsalted butter, room temperature

1½ cups (288 g) granulated sugar

½ cup (105 g) light or dark brown sugar, packed

2 large eggs, room temperature

⅔ cup (160 ml) unsulphured molasses

1 tablespoon (14 g) fresh ginger, finely grated

3 cups (408 g) all-purpose flour

1½ cups (204 g) bread flour

3 teaspoons (8 g) ground ginger

3 teaspoons (13 g) baking soda

2 teaspoons (5 g) cinnamon

1 teaspoon cloves

1 teaspoon sea salt

COOKIE COATING

½ cup (96 g) granulated sugar

To make the Burnt Sugar Ginger, spray a rimmed baking sheet heavily with nonstick spray and set aside.

Add the sugar and ginger to a heavy-bottomed saucepan and use your fingers to massage the ginger into the sugar. Turn the heat to medium high and constantly stir until the sugar liquefies, turns golden brown and no sugar crystals remain. Pour onto the prepared baking sheet and use a spatula to spread evenly until it's about ¼ to ⅛inch (0.7 to 0.3 cm) thick. Set aside for 1 hour to cool and harden. Once cool, turn out onto a cutting board and cut into shards of 1 inch (2.5 cm) and smaller. Careful, they're sharp.

To make the cookie, preheat the oven to 350°F (177°C) and cover several baking sheets with parchment paper.

In an electric stand mixer fitted with the paddle attachment, add the butter, granulated sugar and brown sugar and mix for 4 minutes, or until light and fluffy. With the mixer on low, add in the eggs, one at a time, taking care that each one is fully blended before adding in the next. Make sure to frequently scrape down the sides and bottom of the bowl so that everything is well blended. Add in the molasses and fresh ginger and run the mixer on low for 1 minute more, or until everything is thoroughly combined. Take the bowl out of the mixer and set aside.

In a medium bowl, whisk together the all-purpose flour, bread flour, ground ginger, baking soda, cinnamon, cloves and salt. Add this to the wet ingredients, stirring until just combined and you still see streaks of flour. Add in the burnt sugar shards, stirring until evenly distributed throughout the dough.

To make the cookie coating, place the sugar in a small, shallow bowl. Roll 2 tablespoons (28 g) of dough into a ball and then roll in the sugar to heavily coat. Place on the baking sheet leaving 2 inches (5 cm) between dough balls.

Bake one sheet at a time in the center of the oven for 13 minutes. Let the cookies cool completely on the baking sheet.

PECAN BRITTLE BARK COOKIES

When pecan brittle is just thrown in a cookie as is, it will liquefy and cause the cookie to be a hot, oozy mess. To fix this, the brittle is anchored with some melted chocolate and turned into a bark. I insist that these are moved to the top of your baking list. I mean it.

MAKES 30 COOKIES

PECAN BRITTLE BARK

1 cup (192 g) granulated sugar

⅓ cup (80 ml) corn syrup

¼ cup (60 ml) water

6 tablespoons (86 g) unsalted butter, cut into 6 pieces

1¼ cups (151 g) raw pecans

2 teaspoons (11 ml) real vanilla extract

1 teaspoon baking soda

½ teaspoon sea salt

2¼ cups (270 g) good quality dark chocolate, finely chopped

BARK COOKIES

2 cups (420 g) light brown sugar, packed

8 tablespoons (115 g) unsalted butter, softened

2 large eggs, room temperature

½ cup (118 ml) sunflower seed oil or other neutral oil

1 tablespoon (15 ml) real vanilla extract

2 cups (240 g) white whole-wheat flour

1 cup (136 g) bread flour

2 teaspoons (7 g) baking powder

1 teaspoon baking soda

1 teaspoon sea salt

To make the Pecan Brittle Bark, heavily spray a rimmed baking sheet with nonstick spray and then line with parchment paper. Set aside.

In a medium saucepan, combine the sugar, corn syrup and water over medium heat and let it heat up until the sugar dissolves and no sugar crystals remain. This will take around 5 minutes. Continue with the heat on medium until it gets to 250°F (121°C). Stir in the butter and continue until it reaches 300°F (149°C). Do not let it burn or get too hot. Remove from the heat, stir in the pecans, vanilla, baking soda and salt and immediately spread the mixture over the prepared baking sheet to ¼-inch (0.7-cm) thickness. Cool completely. It should take 1 to 2 hours. Once cool, cut into ½-inch (1.3-cm) chunks. Reserve half of the brittle for another use. Clean the rimmed baking sheet and once again spray with nonstick spray and line with parchment.

In a medium, heat-safe bowl, add the chocolate and set over a medium saucepan of simmering water. Do not let the bowl touch the water or let the water come to a boil. Stir frequently until melted and smooth. Once melted, pour on the prepared baking sheet, using a spatula to smooth to ¼-inch (0.7-cm) thickness and then sprinkle with the brittle. Let cool completely, coarsely chop and then place in the fridge or freezer until ready to use.

To make the cookie, preheat the oven to 350°F (177°C) and cover several baking sheets with parchment paper. Place a rack in the top third of the oven, no less than 6 inches (15 cm) from the heat source.

In an electric stand mixer fitted with the paddle attachment, add the brown sugar and butter and mix on medium for 4 minutes, or until well blended. Scrape down the sides and bottom of the bowl. With the mixer on low, add in the eggs one at a time, making sure each is blended before adding in the next. Add in the oil and vanilla and run the mixer for 1 minute more.

In a medium bowl, whisk together the white whole-wheat flour, bread flour, baking powder, baking soda and sea salt. Add this to the butter mixture and run the machine until barely blended and you still see streaks of flour. Take the bowl out of the mixer and stir in the brittle bark until evenly distributed throughout the dough. Roll 2 tablespoons (28 g) of dough and set on the prepared baking sheet leaving 2 inches (5 cm) between dough balls. Bake one baking sheet at a time for 12 to 13 minutes in the top third of the oven. Let the cookies cool for 5 to 10 minutes on the baking sheet, and then transfer to a rack to finish cooling.

PEANUT BUTTER CUP MERINGUES

Meringues are a great recipe to have in your back pocket. They're extremely versatile to dress up or down. The key to a good meringue is making sure it's whipped properly (so follow the cues below) and also making sure the oven is the correct temperature to bake and dry out the meringue without overbaking and browning. This Peanut Butter Glaze is another keeper. Drizzle it over brownies (page 179), prebake, swirl several figure eights with a knife and you've found another way to satisfy your peanut butter and chocolate cravings!

MAKES 12 (3-INCH [7.7-CM]) MERINGUES

PEANUT BUTTER GLAZE

½ cup (65 g) powdered sugar

1 tablespoon (16 g) natural peanut butter

1 to 2 tablespoons (15 to 30 ml) milk, or more to thin

CHOCOLATE DRIZZLE

⅓ cup (40 g) dark chocolate, finely chopped

MERINGUES

4 large egg whites, room temperature

½ teaspoon cream of tartar

¼ teaspoon sea salt

¾ cup (144 g) granulated sugar

¼ cup (33 g) powdered sugar

Preheat oven to 200°F (93°C). Cover several baking sheets with parchment paper.

To make the Peanut Butter Glaze, in a small bowl, whisk together the powdered sugar, peanut butter and milk until you have a consistency that is thin enough to drizzle, but not so thin it runs off of the meringue. Set aside.

To make the Chocolate Drizzle, in a medium, heat-safe bowl, add the chocolate and set over a medium saucepan of simmering water. Do not let the bowl touch the water or let the water come to a boil. Stir frequently until melted and smooth. Set aside, stirring frequently while it cools.

To make the meringues, in an electric stand mixer fitted with the whisk attachment, add the egg whites, cream of tartar and salt. Make sure the bowl and whisk are freshly cleaned and dried. Whisk on medium until the eggs are frothy and then slowly add in the granulated sugar. Turn the mixer on high and just before you reach stiff peaks, dump in the powdered sugar. Run the mixer on low to combine and then increase to high until you reach stiff peaks, which should take less than a minute depending on the speed of your mixer. The meringue will look glossy and hold its shape when you invert the whisk. The tip of the inverted meringue will be just shy of 12 o'clock. It should also feel smooth when you rub some between your fingers.

Using a 3-tablespoon (42-g) cookie scoop or two spoons, make 12 mounds of meringue on the prepared baking sheet. Drizzle the peanut butter glaze and chocolate over the tops. Use a toothpick or knife to swirl circles at the tops of the meringues...don't dip down too deeply into the meringue; keep it up at the surface. Also, don't do too many swirls, or you'll lose some detail and it will just look messy. You won't use all of the peanut butter glaze, so reserve the rest for another use.

Bake in the center of the oven for 2 hours. Check at some point between 1 and 1½ hours to make sure the meringues aren't browning and are still white. If they're browning, turn off the oven. Let the meringues cool completely inside the oven. This should take several hours.

Meringues are best within several days of making, stored airtight at room temperature. If it is especially humid out allow extra time to dry out in the oven.

TOASTED ALMOND CHOCOLATE MACAROONS

Coconut almond candy bars have always been one of the first things that I dig out of the Halloween bowl. I love them. So, this combination of flavors is totally not unexpected. I did add in puffed rice for some extra texture and flavor. These have flecks of chocolate, crunch from the nuts and chew from the rice. Yum!

MAKES 32 COOKIES

3 large egg whites, room temperature

½ cup (96 g) granulated sugar

1 teaspoon vanilla bean paste or real vanilla extract

¼ teaspoon almond extract

½ teaspoon sea salt

7 ounces (196 g) sweetened condensed milk

5 cups (425 g) sweetened shredded coconut

½ cup (11 g) puffed rice

½ cup (60 g) dark chocolate, coarsely chopped

¼ cup (27 g) almond slivers, toasted

Preheat the oven to 325°F (163°C) and line a baking sheet with parchment paper.

In an electric stand mixer fitted with the whisk attachment, add the egg whites and sugar and beat on medium until frothy and whisk in the vanilla bean paste, almond extract and sea salt. Turn the mixer on high and continue whipping until it holds medium peaks. Invert the whisk, and if the slope of the peak is at 11 o'clock, they're done. They should be smooth and shiny.

In a large bowl, stir together the sweetened condensed milk, coconut, puffed rice, chocolate and almonds. Fold in the egg whites making sure everything is evenly distributed throughout the batter. With damp hands or a 1½-inch (3.7-cm) cookie scoop or two spoons, make 1½-tablespoon (21-g) balls and place on the prepared baking sheet, leaving 1 inch (2.5 cm) between them for air and heat.

Bake for 20 minutes in the center of the oven. Let the cookies cool for 5 minutes on the baking sheet and then transfer to a rack to finish cooling.

TIP

If you're in the mood for something a bit more missionary, just leave out the rice, almonds and chocolate and voilà, you've got a classic macaroon on your hands.

VANILLA CREAM BITES WITH CACAO NIBS

These are deliciously easy, fresh and come together in minutes. Delicate crusts are filled with pastry cream—think chocolate éclairs and cream puffs—and topped with cacao nibs for some crunch and an earthiness that grounds these ethereal little cookies.

MAKES 24 COOKIES

8 tablespoons (115 g) butter, room temperature

7½ ounces (213 g) crème frâiche, room temperature

½ teaspoon sea salt

1¾ cups (238 g) all-purpose flour

VANILLA CREAM

2 large egg yolks

¼ cup (38 g) cornstarch

1¼ cups (296 ml) whole milk

⅓ cup (64 g) granulated sugar

½ vanilla bean, split and scraped or 1 teaspoon real vanilla extract

1 tablespoon (14 g) unsalted butter

CHOCOLATE DRIZZLE

⅔ cup (80 g) dark chocolate, finely chopped

½ tablespoon (7 g) vegetable shortening

2 tablespoons (20 g) cacao nibs, to garnish

To make the crust, in a medium bowl, add the butter, crème frâiche and salt and mash with the back of a fork until well combined. Add in the flour, stirring to combine, making sure there aren't any dry flour patches remaining. Wrap tightly and stash in the fridge for several hours and up to overnight.

Grease a mini-muffin tin with 24 muffin wells and set aside. On a floured surface roll the dough to ¼-inch (0.7-cm) thickness. Use a 2¼-inch-round (5.7-cm) cutter and cut 24 circles out of the dough. Press the dough circles into the muffin tin, gently pressing so they lay flat on the bottom and sides of each well.

Preheat the oven to 350°F (177°C) and bake in the center of the oven for 20 to 25 minutes until puffed and baked through. Use the end of a wooden spoon (or a muddler) to press down the center of each crust to make a well. This is where the cream will go. Let the crust cool for 10 minutes in the muffin tin, and then turn out onto a cooling rack to finish cooling.

To make the Vanilla Cream, in a small bowl, stir the egg yolks and cornstarch until a paste forms. Set aside.

In a medium heavy-bottomed saucepan, add the milk, granulated sugar and vanilla over medium heat, stirring until the sugar dissolves. Add ½ cup (118 ml) of the warmed milk slowly to the egg yolk mixture, whisking the entire time. Once well blended, grab a strainer and strain the egg yolk mixture into the saucepan. Turn up the heat to medium high and constantly whisk until the mixture has thickened. This should take just a couple of minutes. Take it off of the heat and stir in the butter until melted. If it develops any lumps you may want to strain again for the smoothest consistency. Immediately scoop the mixture into a clean bowl and cover the surface directly with plastic wrap. This will keep a scab from forming. Place in the fridge until chilled through.

To assemble, fill a pastry bag fitted with a round tip with the vanilla cream and fill each crust with a dollop. You could also just spoon the cream into each crust.

To make the Chocolate Drizzle, in a medium, heat-safe bowl, add the chocolate and shortening and set over a medium saucepan of simmering water. Do not let it touch the water or let the water come to a boil. Set a towel on the countertop and once melted, remove from the heat, set on top of the towel and continue stirring until cooled. Drizzle the chocolate over the tops of each cookie cup and sprinkle with a few cacao nibs. Serve immediately or store in a single layer in an airtight container in the fridge until ready to eat. These are best eaten the day they are made.

HAZELNUT COCOA MACARONS

I am not one to insist on weighing all of your ingredients while baking...I think it's simply unrealistic and most people can't be bothered. However, macarons are one of the exceptions. There is a degree of precision needed for macaron success. The other component is technique. So, follow the instructions to the letter, and I recommend measuring the ingredients by weight. Each time you make them, you'll build on what you've learned and they'll get better and better. Promise.

MAKES 42 MACARONS

1½ cups plus 2½ tablespoons (215 g) powdered sugar

1½ cups plus scant 1 tablespoon (125 g) finely ground hazelnut flour or meal

2 tablespoons (10 g) dark unsweetened cocoa powder

Roughly 4 large egg whites (130 g)

¼ teaspoon cream of tartar

½ cup (105 g) granulated sugar

To make the cookies, cover several baking sheets with parchment paper. Prepare your pastry bag by placing a round pastry tip in the bottom and place in a large glass or vase to make it easier to fill. Prepare one more pastry bag with a round tip that you'll use later for the filling.

Add half of the powdered sugar to a food processor fitted with the blade attachment and top with the hazelnut meal and then the remainder of the powdered sugar and the cocoa powder. Pulse 6 to 8 times until no hazelnut meal is visible. Sift several times, discarding any large bits left in the sifter. Set aside.

In an electric stand mixer fitted with the whisk attachment, add the egg whites and cream of tartar. Make sure the bowl and whisk are freshly cleaned and dried. Whisk on medium until the eggs are frothy and then slowly add in the granulated sugar. Turn the mixer on high until you reach stiff peaks. You'll know it's ready when you invert the whisk and the meringue holds its shape. The tip of the inverted meringue will be just shy of 12 o'clock. It should also feel smooth when you rub some between your fingers.

Sift the dry ingredients one more time into the meringue in three batches, folding and mixing between each one. It should take around 20 to 25 folds for everything to get mixed together. Then spread the batter up the sides of the bowl and scoop it back down to the bottom. Repeat this about three or four times or until the mixture starts to slowly slump back down the sides of the bowl. Scoop the mixture into your prepared pastry bag and cut the bottom tip off.

Hold the pastry tip just above the baking sheet, and then press out the batter into the shape of a circle the size of a nickel, pause for a second at the top and then quickly pull the pastry tip off to the side. You want the tops as smooth as possible. The macarons will spread a wee bit so leave about 1½ to 2 inches (3.7 to 5 cm) between each. Tap the pans 4 times on the counter to release any trapped bubbles and let sit for 20 to 45 minutes until they become dull, and when gently touched no batter is transferred to your finger; this time will vary depending on local humidity.

(continued)

HAZELNUT COCOA MACARONS (CONTINUED)

HAZELNUT FILLING

½ cup (85 g) raw hazelnuts, coarsely chopped

1 tablespoon (12 g) granulated sugar

¼ cup (30 g) semisweet chocolate, finely chopped

8 tablespoons (115 g) unsalted butter, cut into 8 pieces

2 tablespoons (30 ml) heavy whipping cream

¼ teaspoon sea salt

1 cup (130 g) powdered sugar

Preheat the oven to 320°F (160°C) and bake the macarons for 11 minutes or until they lift easily off of the parchment. If they don't easily come off, add 1 minute more of bake time until they do. Take care not to overbake them—they shouldn't darken or show any color change in the oven. Let cool completely.

To make the filling, in a food processor fitted with the blade attachment, add the hazelnuts and granulated sugar and run until the mixture is combined, about 3 minutes.

In a medium, heat-safe bowl, add the chocolate and set over a medium saucepan of simmering water. Do not let the bowl touch the water or let the water come to a boil. Stir until the chocolate melts. Add in the butter and whipping cream. Blend in the hazelnut mixture and finish with a pinch of salt. Set a towel on the counter and set the bowl on top. Let cool for 15 minutes, stirring frequently. Once cooled, stir in the powdered sugar. The mixture will be thick. Transfer to the prepared pastry bag and once cool, pipe the filling onto half of the macarons and then top with another macaron of equal size.

TIP

- See Peppermint Candy Macrons (page 127) for more macron-making tips!
- Use finely ground, blanched hazelnut meal and don't skip sifting. You want the tops of the macarons to be as smooth as possible, and I've found hazelnut flour or meal to be particularly lumpy.

VANILLA BEAN THUMBPRINT COOKIES
WITH DULCE DE LECHE

These are pretty easy cookies to throw together, the only high maintenance component is that you need to make the dulce de leche in advance so that it has time to cool. Other than that, this is a sweet, delicate cookie with the dulce giving it mega jazz hands.

MAKES 35 COOKIES

DULCE DE LECHE

1 (14-ounce [392-ml]) can sweetened condensed milk

VANILLA SUGAR

½ cup (96 g) granulated sugar

½ vanilla bean, split and scraped

THUMBPRINT COOKIE

16 tablespoons (230 g) unsalted butter, room temperature

1 cup (192 g) granulated sugar

1 large egg yolk, room temperature

1 tablespoon (15 ml) milk

½ vanilla bean, split and scraped or 1 teaspoon real vanilla extract

2⅓ cups (317 g) all-purpose flour

½ teaspoon baking powder

½ teaspoon sea salt

¼ cup (33 g) powdered sugar

To make the Dulce de Leche, take the label off of the condensed milk can and place the can in a deep, heavy-bottomed Dutch oven and cover with cold water until it covers the can by 2 inches (5 cm). Bring to a boil and then reduce to a simmer for 3 hours. Check every 30 minutes or so, adding more water to keep it 2 inches (5 cm) above the can. Remove from the pot with tongs and set on the counter to cool completely; this will take at least several hours. Do not open while hot.

To make the Vanilla Sugar, place the sugar and the vanilla bean seeds in a food processor fitted with the blade. Run the machine for 20 seconds to combine. Place half of the sugar in an airtight container with the vanilla bean pod and reserve for a later use. Place the other half in a small, shallow bowl and set aside.

To make the Thumbprint Cookies, preheat the oven to 350°F (177°C) and line several baking sheets with parchment paper.

In an electric stand mixer fitted with the paddle attachment, add the butter and granulated sugar and run the machine for 4 minutes on medium until smooth and well blended. Add in the egg yolk, milk and vanilla and run the machine for several minutes. The mixture may appear curdled.

In a medium bowl, whisk together the flour, baking powder and salt. Add this to the butter mixture and run the machine until the dough comes together, about 1 minute. Roll 1 tablespoon (14 g) of dough into a ball and then roll in the vanilla sugar. Set on the baking sheet and press your thumb in the center. There will be some small cracks, press them back together if you'd like or just let them be. Leave about 2 inches (5 cm) between dough balls as these will spread a bit. Chill for 30 minutes in the freezer or 60 minutes in the refrigerator.

(continued)

Bake one sheet at a time in the center of the oven for 12 minutes. Take the cookies out of the oven and with the round end of a wooden spoon (or a muddler) press down the center of the cookie one more time. Let them cool on the baking sheet for 5 minutes and then transfer to a rack to finish cooling.

Once cool, sift powdered sugar over the tops of the cookies and put about 1 teaspoon of dulce de leche in the center well of each cookie.

TIPS

- You'll have leftover dulce de leche, and I highly suggest you drizzle it over some ice cream.
- To get the vanilla seeds, use a sharp paring knife to split the vanilla bean down the middle and then use the back side of your knife to scrape the seeds out of the pod. You will also have leftover vanilla bean sugar of which you could use wherever you might use regular sugar—in coffee, making more cookies, sprinkled over a cupcake, or my personal favorite: to rim your Friday night cocktail.
- These cookies are best stored in a single layer as the dulce de leche will never set or firm up.

FIVE-SPICE CRANBERRY MOONCAKE COOKIES

I'm so obsessed with the way mooncakes look. Here, I use my sturdy sugar cookie recipe, a favorite flavor combination (cranberries and five-spice powder) and add in some white chocolate, nuts and a citrus glaze.

MAKES 23 COOKIES

FIVE-SPICE FILLING

¾ cup (75 g) fresh or frozen cranberries

¼ cup (41 g) dried tart cherries

3 tablespoons (41 g) light brown sugar, packed

3 tablespoons (45 ml) water

½ teaspoon five-spice powder

½ cup (58 g) raw walnuts or pecans or pistachios, coarsely chopped

½ cup (60 g) white chocolate, coarsely chopped

MOONCAKE COOKIES

24 tablespoons (345 g) unsalted butter, cut into 24 pieces, room temperature

1½ cups (288 g) granulated sugar

2 large eggs, room temperature

1 large egg yolk, room temperature

2 teaspoons (11 ml) real vanilla extract

2 cups (272 g) bread flour

2 cups (272 g) all-purpose flour

1 teaspoon sea salt

GLAZE

1 cup (130 g) powdered sugar

3 tablespoons (45 ml) milk

1 tablespoon (15 ml) fresh orange juice

To make the Five-Spice Filling, in a medium heavy-bottomed saucepan, add the cranberries, cherries, brown sugar, water and five-spice powder and bring to a boil. Reduce to a simmer, stirring frequently for about 6 minutes, or until the cranberries have popped and most of the liquid has evaporated. Set aside to cool completely.

In a food processor fitted with the blade, add the walnuts and run the machine until they are finely chopped. Add in the chocolate and pulse several times until the chocolate is finely chopped and the mixture is blended. Finally add in the cooled cranberry mixture and pulse the machine to combine. Place the mixture in the fridge to firm up some more while you make your cookie.

To make the cookies, in an electric stand mixer fitted with the paddle attachment, add the butter and sugar and mix on medium until light and fluffy, about 4 minutes. Scrape down the sides and bottom of the bowl and add in the eggs and egg yolk, one at a time, making sure to completely blend the first before adding the next. Add in the vanilla and blend for 1 minute more, again scraping down the sides and bottom.

In a large bowl, whisk together the bread flour, all-purpose flour and sea salt. Add to the butter mixture and run the machine for 1 minute more or until just blended. Separate the dough into 23, roughly 3-tablespoon-sized (42-g) balls. It's messy. Sorry.

To assemble, cover a baking sheet with parchment paper. Press your thumb in the center of the cookie dough ball and make enough space for the filling. Put about 1 teaspoon of filling in there and then press the dough over to enclose it. It's ok if the dough gets stained from the cranberries, it looks pretty once baked and I actually found myself purposely making it happen. Just make sure the actual filling is encapsulated by the dough.

Lightly flour a clean surface as well as the dough ball and the mooncake mold. Press a 5¾ x 2½-inch (14.5 x 6.5–cm) mold, or cookie stamp, down on the dough ball until it meets some resistance. Gently tap the mold on the counter to release the mooncake cookie and place on the prepared baking sheet leaving 1½ inches (3.7 cm) between cookies. Freeze the cookies for 1 hour or refrigerate for 2 hours.

Preheat the oven to 350°F (177°C). Bake one sheet at a time in the center of the oven for 17 to 18 minutes. Let the cookies cool completely on the baking sheet.

To make the glaze, once the cookies are cool, in a small bowl whisk together the powdered sugar, milk and orange juice. Invert the mooncakes into the glaze, letting the excess drip back into the bowl. Scrape the side of your finger over the surface of the mooncake to remove any excess glaze.

LEMONY WHITE CHOCOLATE TRUFFLES

It's amazing that so few ingredients and so little effort can result in something so glorious. At any special occasion when I was growing up my grandmother (Granny Pete) would give the grandchildren a box of See's chocolates. I absolutely loved the lemon truffle...and this tastes exactly like that filling. At least that's what my sister said when she tasted them. These are so sinfully easy and so freaking cute that they demand to be part of your repertoire.

MAKES 35 TRUFFLES

1½ cups (180 g) good quality white chocolate (not chips), finely chopped

⅓ cup (79 ml) heavy whipping cream, warm

3 tablespoons (43 g) unsalted butter, room temperature

1 tablespoon (9 g) lemon zest

1 teaspoon fresh lemon juice

TRUFFLE COATING

½ cup (96 g) granulated sugar

2 tablespoons (19 g) lemon zest

½ cup (65 g) powdered sugar

Place the chocolate in a heat-safe bowl, pour the warm cream over and add the butter, zest and juice. Cover with plastic wrap and set aside for 5 minutes. Uncover and stir until smooth and glossy. Cover loosely with plastic wrap and set on the counter. The mixture should firm up enough to roll in about 2 hours.

Cover a baking sheet with parchment paper.

To make the coating, place the granulated sugar and the lemon zest in a food processor fitted with the blade. Run the machine for 20 seconds to combine. Place the mixture in a shallow bowl and set aside. Put the powdered sugar in another shallow bowl.

Using a melon baller or small scoop, scrape up 2 teaspoons (9 g) of chocolate and mold into a ball. Roll half of the balls in the powdered sugar and the other half in the lemon sugar.

For storage, first chill the truffles in a single layer. Once set, store in the fridge in an airtight container, lined in parchment with parchment separating each layer of truffles, for several weeks.

CHOCOLATE CHERRY CHEESECAKE THUMBPRINTS

If you're a fan of traditional chocolate cherry cheesecake, you'll love these little bites. The chocolate cookie base comes together easily and is topped with a light cream cheese mixture and a dollop of cherry jam. You can use the cherry jam from the Cherry Streusel Jam Bars (page 183) or grab your favorite store-bought version. I prefer the ones that are chunky and just a little bit drizzly. If you need to make these ahead of time bake the cookies and prepare the cream cheese filling in advance and store separately (with the filling in the fridge) and assemble the cookies just prior to serving.

MAKES 30 COOKIES

THUMBPRINT COOKIE

¾ cup (90 g) dark chocolate, finely chopped

16 tablespoons (230 g) unsalted butter, cut into 16 pieces, room temperature

1½ cups (288 g) granulated sugar

2 large eggs, room temperature

1½ teaspoons (7 ml) real vanilla extract

1⅔ cups (226 g) all-purpose flour

⅔ cup (56 g) unsweetened dark (Dutch process) cocoa powder

½ teaspoon sea salt

½ teaspoon baking powder

COOKIE COATING

½ cup (96 g) granulated sugar or sparkling sugar

CHEESECAKE FILLING

6 ounces (170 g) cream cheese, room temperature

¼ cup (33 g) powdered sugar

2 tablespoons (30 ml) milk

½ cup (6 oz) cherry jam (page 183), or store-bought

To make the cookies, in a medium, heat-safe bowl, add the chocolate and set over a medium saucepan of simmering water. Do not let the bowl touch the water or let the water come to a boil. Stir frequently until melted and smooth. Once melted, turn off the burner and leave the chocolate in the bowl over the saucepan.

In an electric stand mixer fitted with the paddle attachment, add the butter and sugar and mix on medium for 4 minutes, or until light and fluffy. With the mixer on low, add in the eggs one at a time, making sure the first is well blended before adding in the next. With the mixer still on low, slowly stream in the chocolate. Add in the vanilla and mix for 1 minute more. Scrape the sides and bottom of the bowl to make sure everything is incorporated.

In a medium bowl, whisk together the flour, cocoa powder, sea salt and baking powder. Add to the butter mixture and mix on low until the dough comes together. Scrape the sides and bottom of the bowl to make sure everything is well blended and there are no light-colored streaks of butter remaining. Wrap the dough tightly and chill in the fridge for 1 hour.

Preheat your oven to 350°F (177°C) and line several baking sheets with parchment paper.

For the coating, place the sugar in a small, shallow bowl.

Roll 1½ tablespoons (21 g) of dough into a ball and then roll in the sugar. Set on the prepared baking sheet, leaving 2 inches (5 cm) of space between dough balls.

Press down with your thumb in the middle of each dough ball. Chill for 20 minutes in the freezer or 40 minutes in the fridge. Bake one sheet at a time in the middle of the oven for 13 to 15 minutes. Take the thumbprints out of the oven and press the center down with the round end of a wooden spoon (or a muddler) and let cool for 5 minutes, and then transfer to a rack to finish cooling.

To make the filling, in a medium bowl, stir together the cream cheese, powdered sugar and milk until smooth. Fill the well of each cookie with the cream cheese filling and then top with about a teaspoon of cherry jam. These are best eaten the same day they are baked.

DAZZLING
DROP COOKIES

Drop cookies are the perfect cookies to satisfy mid-week cravings because they can usually be quickly mixed up and out of the oven in no time. Sometimes I mix them up and coordinate oven time with commercials so I don't have to hit pause on the television. These cookies have their origins in the classics, but they are totally unique in their combinations of flavors. And while their technique is often simple, it's the flavors that really make these sing. Instead of making typical snowballs or Mexican Wedding Cookies, I used hazelnuts and infused them with major mint chip vibes for the Hazelnut Mint Chip Coolers (page 101).

Come September I'm always looking for ways to bake with pumpkin, as I love the flavor and texture it lends to sweet treats. This chapter has two pumpkin-based cookies: the Brown Butter Pumpkin Cookies (page 94) and the Chocolate Pumpkin Swirl Cookies (page 97).

The Lemon Poppy Seed Cookies (page 82) are just as good during the summer as they are at the height of citrus season. I'm thinking we should both try these with grapefruit...or maybe blood orange? Just replace the lemon citrus with another citrus in a 1:1 ratio. And if you're looking to warm up your mornings AND eat cookies for breakfast, I hope you'll start eating the Oatmeal, Blueberry and Quinoa Breakfast Cookies. Please note that puffed quinoa needs to be a staple in your cupboard from this moment forward.

Let's drop some cookies, shall we?

LEMON POPPY SEED COOKIES

Have you acquainted yourself with lemon sugar? Lime sugar? Any citrus sugar for that matter? You basically pulse (or aggressively chop) together granulated sugar and citrus zest. It makes the most magical mixture to rim cocktail glasses, sprinkle aggressively over cupcakes or in this instance, roll your cookie dough balls. I often love soft and chewy cookies, but these have a little more crisp and chew, without being hard. I wouldn't do that to you. But the best part is: these contain a ginormous burst of bright lemon. It's like a citrus party in your mouth...really not to be missed.

MAKES 24 COOKIES

8 tablespoons (115 g) unsalted butter, room temperature

¾ cup (158 g) light brown sugar, packed

¾ cup (144 g) granulated sugar

2 large eggs, room temperature

1 large egg yolk, room temperature

¾ cup (177 ml) sunflower seed oil or other neutral oil

3 tablespoons (28 g) lemon zest

1 tablespoon (15 ml) fresh lemon juice

2¾ cups (375 g) bread flour

1 tablespoon (8 g) poppy seeds

2 teaspoons (6 g) cream of tartar

1 teaspoon baking soda

1 teaspoon sea salt

½ teaspoon cinnamon

LEMON SUGAR

⅓ cup (64 g) granulated sugar

2 tablespoons (19 g) lemon zest

2 tablespoons (14 g) powdered sugar

To make the cookies, in an electric stand mixer fitted with the paddle, add the butter, brown sugar, granulated sugar and mix on medium for 4 minutes, or until light and fluffy. Add in the eggs and egg yolk one at a time, making sure each is well blended before adding in the next. Scrape down the sides and bottom of the bowl and then add in the oil, lemon zest and lemon juice and mix for 1 minute more.

In a medium-size bowl, whisk together the bread flour, poppy seeds, cream of tartar, baking soda, salt and cinnamon. Pour the flour mixture into the butter mixture and mix on low until the dough just comes together. Wrap tightly and stash in the fridge for several hours, or until the dough has firmed up.

To make the lemon sugar, in a food processor, pulse together the granulated sugar, lemon zest and powdered sugar until blended, but not fine.

Take the dough out of the fridge and roll about 1½ tablespoons (21 g) of dough between your palms into a nice ball. Take note: the dough is a bit sticky. Give the dough ball a generous coating of the lemon sugar and set it on the prepared baking sheet, allowing 2 inches (5 cm) between dough balls. Chill the dough balls in the freezer for 10 to 15 minutes or fridge for 20 to 30 minutes. Don't skip this step.

Preheat your oven to 350°F (177°C). Make sure a rack is in the top third of the oven at least 6 inches (15 cm) from the heat source. Cover your baking sheets with parchment paper.

Take the dough balls directly from the freezer or fridge to the top rack of the oven and bake one sheet at a time for 12 minutes. Let them cool on the cookie sheet for 5 minutes, and then let the cookies finish cooling on a cooling rack.

OATMEAL, BLUEBERRY AND
PUFFED QUINOA BREAKFAST COOKIES

Don't think this cookie is just blueberries and oatmeal. Consider it a blank canvas for your taste buds and what's in season. Fresh cherries with almonds, yes please! What about raspberries and macadamia nuts? Or peaches and pecans? The combinations are endless. This is the perfect cookie dough to freeze so you can enjoy a fresh, warm cookie in the morning. Place the dough balls on a parchment covered baking sheet in a single layer and freeze for several hours or until solid. Store in an airtight container. Take directly from the freezer to the pre-heated oven, adding several extra minutes to the bake time.

MAKES 30 COOKIES

¾ cup (177 ml) good quality olive oil

¼ cup (60 g) 2-percent Greek yogurt

¾ cup (158 g) light brown sugar, packed

¼ cup (48 g) granulated sugar

3 large eggs, room temperature

1 tablespoon (9 g) lemon zest

2 teaspoons (11 ml) pure vanilla extract

1 teaspoon almond extract

1½ cups (180 g) white whole-wheat flour

⅓ cup (45 g) all-purpose flour

1½ teaspoons (4 g) cinnamon

2 teaspoons (7 g) baking powder

1 teaspoon baking soda

1 teaspoon sea salt

½ teaspoon freshly grated nutmeg

2 cups (182 g) old-fashioned rolled oats

1 cup (60 g) puffed quinoa

½ cup (61 g) raw almonds, toasted and chopped

3 cups (426 g) fresh blueberries

In a large bowl, whisk together the oil, Greek yogurt, brown sugar and granulated sugar until smooth. Add the eggs, lemon zest, vanilla and almond extract and whisk until smooth.

In a medium bowl, whisk together the white whole-wheat flour, all-purpose flour, cinnamon, baking powder, baking soda, sea salt and nutmeg. Dump into the butter mixture and mix until the cookie dough is barely blended; you'll still see streaks of flour. Add in the oats, quinoa and almonds and mix until just combined. Fold in the blueberries. If the dough is too sticky to roll, cover tightly and set in the fridge for 20 minutes or until it has firmed up.

Preheat your oven to 350°F (177°C). Make sure you have a rack in the top third of your oven 6 inches (15 cm) from the heat source. Line a baking sheet with parchment paper.

Roll the dough into balls of about ¼ cup (57 g) of dough and allow 2 inches (5 cm) of space between the balls. Wet your hands and press the dough down so they are discs.

Bake one sheet at a time in the top third of the oven for 15 minutes. Allow to cool completely on the baking sheet before serving.

TIPS

· Pick an olive oil that tastes delicious to you out of the bottle, as some of the flavor will carry through in the final taste of the cookie.

· These cookies will soften over time. Place in a preheated 350°F (177°C) oven and warm for 5 minutes to toast back up.

OLD-FASHIONED ICED OATMEAL COOKIES

We almost always had homemade cookies in our house growing up, but if we happened to have store-bought cookies, they were often iced old-fashioned oatmeal cookies. Here, I re-created that classic store-bought cookie, but with a small hint of cardamom and flecks of vanilla bean in the glaze to kick things up a notch.

MAKES 36 COOKIES

8 tablespoons (115 g) unsalted butter

⅓ cup (79 ml) sunflower seed oil or other neutral oil

1¼ cups (263 g) light brown sugar, packed

¼ cup (48 g) granulated sugar

2 large eggs, room temperature

1 tablespoon (15 ml) real vanilla extract

2 cups (182 g) old-fashioned rolled oats

1¼ cups (170 g) all-purpose flour

¾ cup (90 g) white whole-wheat flour

3 teaspoons (11 g) baking powder

2 teaspoons (5 g) cinnamon

1½ teaspoons (7 g) sea salt

½ teaspoon baking soda

½ teaspoon cardamom

½ teaspoon nutmeg

GLAZE

1½ cups (195 g) powdered sugar

2 tablespoons (30 ml) milk

½ vanilla bean, split lengthwise and scraped

To make the cookies, preheat your oven to 375°F (190°C) and place a rack in the top third of the oven, at least 6 inches (15 cm) away from the heat source. Cover several baking sheets with parchment paper.

Put the butter in a large, microwave-safe bowl and microwave on high for 30 to 60 seconds, or until melted. Microwave times vary, so check periodically. Set aside to cool a minute. Once cooled slightly, whisk in the oil, brown sugar, granulated sugar, eggs and vanilla.

In a high-speed blender or food processor fitted with the blade, pulse the oats until they are coarsely chopped. Some bits will be fine and dusty, others more substantial; this is fine. Add the oats to a medium bowl and whisk with the all-purpose flour, whole-wheat flour, baking powder, cinnamon, sea salt, baking soda, cardamom and nutmeg. Pour this into the butter mixture and stir until just combined. Let sit on the counter for 10 minutes (the dough will be easier to roll). Gently roll 1½ tablespoons (21 g) of dough into a ball and place on a baking sheet 2 inches (5 cm) apart from each other.

Bake one sheet at a time in the top third of the oven for 8 minutes, then take the sheet out of the oven and drop the baking sheet twice on the counter, and place back in the oven for 1 minute more (for a total bake time of 9 minutes). Let the cookies cool on the baking sheet for 5 minutes, and then transfer to a cooling rack.

To make the glaze, in a medium bowl, whisk together the powdered sugar, milk and vanilla bean seeds. Add more milk in small 1 teaspoon increments, if necessary, to get the desired consistency. You want the glaze pretty thick so that it shows up as opaque and sits on the top of the cookie rather than drizzles in all of the nooks and crannies. Lightly dip the tops of the cookies into the glaze, taking care not to submerge the cookies—you want to see the crevasses. Hold the cookie upside down for a minute to let the excess fall back into the bowl.

TIPS

- Do not replace white whole-wheat flour with regular whole-wheat flour as it will make the cookie too dense.
- Banging the cookies on the counter flattens the cookie, giving it the traditional "old-fashioned" oatmeal cookie look.

BROWN BUTTER MUSCOVADO SNICKERDOODLES

This is one of the few cookies that I brought over from my blog because I just wouldn't be nice if I hoarded it only for my online readers. Snickerdoodles on their own are damn near the perfect cookie. But when you swap in brown butter for regular and then amp up the toffee and caramel notes even more by adding in dark muscovado in place of half of the sugar, the resulting cookie is just freaking delicious. My dad is one of those people that loves things the way they've always been, so I was hesitant to have him taste this cookie. But he loved it! And even if you are a traditional snickerdoodle lover, you will absolutely love the combination of flavors in here.

MAKES 24 COOKIES

8 tablespoons (115 g) unsalted butter

¾ cup (178 ml) sunflower seed oil or other neutral oil

¾ cup (158 g) dark muscovado sugar, packed

¾ cup (144 g) granulated sugar

3 teaspoons (15 ml) real vanilla extract

2 large eggs, room temperature

1¾ cups (239 g) bread flour

1 cup (136 g) all-purpose flour

2 teaspoons (6 g) cream of tartar

1 teaspoon baking soda

1 teaspoon sea salt

COOKIE COATING

¼ cup (48 g) granulated sugar

1 teaspoon cinnamon

1 teaspoon cardamom

Put the butter in a medium, heavy-bottomed saucepan and melt over medium heat. Once melted, crank up the heat to medium high. Stand by, stirring and watching. Small golden bits will start to settle on the bottom of the pan and you'll notice a caramel smell. This should take around 3 to 5 minutes. Once this happens, take the butter off of the heat and pour it into a medium, heat-safe bowl to cool a bit. After several minutes, add the oil, muscovado sugar, granulated sugar, vanilla and eggs to the browned butter. Whisk together until thoroughly blended. It will be thick and sludge-like. Break up any large chunks of the muscovado.

In a medium-sized bowl, whisk together the bread flour, all-purpose flour, cream of tartar, baking soda and salt. Pour this into the butter mixture. Don't overmix, but make sure everything gets blended together well. I like to mix until the flour just disappears. Wrap tightly and stash in the fridge for 30 minutes until firm.

To make the cookie coating, in a small, shallow bowl, whisk together the granulated sugar, cinnamon and cardamom. Take the dough out of the fridge and roll about 1½ tablespoons (21 g) of dough between your palms into a nice ball. Give the dough ball a generous coating of the sugar-spice mixture and set it on the cookie sheet. Make sure there are about 2 inches (5 cm) between each dough ball, allowing space for spreading while baking. For a puffier cookie, place the baking sheet with the coated dough balls in the freezer for 15 minutes or the fridge for 30 minutes. Otherwise bake immediately.

Preheat your oven to 350°F (177°C). Make sure a rack is in the top third of the oven at least 6 inches (15 cm) from the heat source. Bake one sheet at a time in the top third of the oven for 11 to 12 minutes. Let them cool on the baking sheet for 10 minutes and then finish cooling on a rack.

OVERNIGHT BANANA BREAD
CHOCOLATE CHIP COOKIES

I knew it. You've been looking for one more recipe to use ripe bananas for. This is one of those cookie recipes where you have to let the dough sit in the fridge overnight—the dough is easier to roll into balls and it gets more banana flavor while it rests. If you'd like even more banana vibes, throw in ½ cup (113 g) of small diced ripe (not overripe) banana to the mix when you add in the chocolate and walnuts.

MAKES 24 COOKIES

1½ cups (330 g) light or dark brown sugar, packed

½ cup (113 g) mashed ripe banana (about 1 banana)

8 tablespoons (115 g) unsalted butter, room temperature

⅓ cup (79 ml) sunflower seed oil or other neutral oil

2 large eggs, room temperature

1 tablespoon (15 ml) real vanilla extract

2 cups (272 g) all-purpose flour

¾ cup (80 g) oat flour*

1 teaspoon baking powder

1 teaspoon baking soda

1½ teaspoons (7 g) sea salt

½ teaspoon nutmeg

1½ cups (180 g) dark chocolate, coarsely chopped or chips

1 cup (122 g) walnuts, toasted and finely chopped

*Grind 1 cup (91 g) of old-fashioned rolled oats in a food processor or high-speed blender until it's mostly smooth like flour with some coarser bits throughout.

In an electric stand mixer fitted with the paddle attachment, add your brown sugar, banana and butter and mix on medium for several minutes or until completely blended. With the mixer on low, add in the oil, the eggs one at a time, not adding the next until the first is fully blended, and then finally the vanilla. Be sure to scrape the sides and bottom of the bowl so that everything is incorporated. Take the bowl out of the mixer and set aside.

In another medium bowl, whisk together the all-purpose flour, oat flour, baking powder, baking soda, sea salt and nutmeg. Add this to the banana mixture and stir until barely combined. Add the chocolate and walnuts and continue to blend until just combined. Wrap tightly and stash in the fridge for 12 hours or more, ideally overnight and up to several days. Don't skip this step as you will develop some exciting banana flavor during this time.

Preheat your oven to 350°F (177°C). Cover several baking sheets with parchment paper. Use roughly 2 tablespoons (28 g) of dough per cookie and gently roll the dough into a ball. Set the dough balls on the prepared baking sheet, 2 inches (5 cm) apart.

Bake one sheet at a time in the center of the oven for 11 to 12 minutes. They will appear slightly underdone, that's perfect. Let them cool for about 10 minutes on the baking sheet, and then transfer to the cooling rack.

TIPS

- I'm not of the belief that the best bananas for baking are the ones where the peel has gone completely black. Instead, use bananas that are ripe, still slightly firm and the peel is a combination of yellow with brown spots.

- Similar to banana bread, these won't last long at room temperature because of the moisture from the banana. Enjoy within a day or two or stash in the fridge to keep them longer.

MOLASSES GINGER CRACKLES

If you're feeling like exploring muscovado sugar and cookies, this is the place to do it. I love how the sparkling sugar crunches when you bite down on the cookie. This is one of those cookie doughs that truly benefits from time spent in the fridge. Allow time for the dough to rest and firm up before trying to roll into balls.

MAKES 24 COOKIES

¾ cup (158 g) dark brown sugar or muscovado, packed

8 tablespoons (115 g) unsalted butter, room temperature

¼ cup (48 g) granulated sugar

⅓ cup (80 ml) unsulphured molasses

⅓ cup (79 ml) sunflower seed oil or other neutral oil

2 large eggs, room temperature

1 large egg yolk, room temperature

2 tablespoons (29 g) freshly grated ginger

1 tablespoon (15 ml) real vanilla extract

2 cups (272 g) all-purpose flour

1 cup (136 g) bread flour

1 tablespoon (8 g) ground ginger

2 teaspoons (6 g) baking soda

2 teaspoons (5 g) cinnamon

1 teaspoon cloves

1 teaspoon cardamom

1 teaspoon sea salt

COOKIE COATING
½ cup (96 g) sparkling sugar

In an electric-stand mixer fitted with the paddle attachment, beat the brown sugar, butter and granulated sugar on medium until completely blended and creamy, about 4 minutes. Scrape the sides and bottom of the bowl to make sure everything is incorporated. Add in the molasses, oil, eggs, egg yolk, fresh ginger and vanilla and mix on low for several minutes until thoroughly blended. Take the bowl out of the stand mixer.

In a medium bowl, whisk together the all-purpose flour, bread flour, ground ginger, baking soda, cinnamon, cloves, cardamom and sea salt. Pour into the butter-molasses mixture and fold with a spatula until just combined. Wrap tightly and place in the fridge for at least several hours or up to several days. This dough is sticky, do not skip this step.

When ready to bake, preheat the oven to 350°F (177°C) and cover your baking sheets with parchment paper. Place the sparkling sugar in a shallow bowl.

Gently roll 2 tablespoons (28 g) of dough into a ball and then roll in the sparkling sugar. Cover each dough ball completely and do not shake off the excess. Place on the cookie sheet, allowing about 2 inches (5 cm) between each dough ball. Press each dough ball down slightly to form a disc.

Bake one sheet at a time for 11 minutes in the center of the oven. You want to slightly undercook these. Allow the cookies to cool on the sheet for 5 to 10 minutes, then transfer to a cooling rack.

TIP
If you don't have any sparkling sugar available, substitute regular granulated sugar.

BROWN BUTTER PUMPKIN COOKIES

As soon as it's "Baking with Pumpkin Season" (I'm talking September 1st), you need to start making this cookie. And keep baking it through to Thanksgiving. These cookies taste like spiced pumpkin clouds with the perfect tangy frosting.

MAKES 32 COOKIES

8 tablespoons (115 g) unsalted butter

½ cup (118 ml) sunflower seed oil or other neutral oil

⅓ cup (79 ml) pumpkin puree (not pumpkin pie filling)

¾ cup (158 g) dark muscovado sugar or dark brown sugar, packed

¾ cup (144 g) granulated sugar

3 teaspoons (15 ml) real vanilla extract

2 large eggs, room temperature

1¾ cups (239 g) bread flour

1 cup (136 g) all-purpose flour

2 teaspoons (7 g) baking powder

1 teaspoon baking soda

1 teaspoon sea salt

1 teaspoon cinnamon

¼ teaspoon nutmeg

¼ teaspoon cloves

¼ teaspoon ginger

COOKIE COATING

¼ cup (48 g) granulated sugar

1 teaspoon cinnamon

¼ teaspoon nutmeg

¼ teaspoon cloves

¼ teaspoon ginger

CREAM CHEESE FROSTING

2 tablespoons (29 g) unsalted butter, room temperature

3 ounces (85 g) cream cheese, room temperature

2½ cups (325 g) powdered sugar

1 teaspoon ground cinnamon

¼ teaspoon nutmeg

2 to 3 tablespoons (30 to 45 ml) milk, or more to thin

Put the butter in a medium, heavy-bottomed saucepan over medium heat and melt. Once melted, crank up the heat to medium-high. Stir until small golden bits start to settle on the bottom of the pan and it smells nutty and caramel-y. This should take around 3 to 5 minutes. Remove from the heat before the bits turn dark brown and pour the butter into a large, heat-safe bowl to cool slightly. Add the oil, pumpkin, muscovado sugar, granulated sugar, vanilla and eggs, whisking well with each addition until thoroughly blended. The mixture will be thick and sludge-like. Break up any large chunks of the muscovado.

In a medium bowl, whisk together the bread flour, all-purpose flour, baking powder, baking soda, salt, cinnamon, nutmeg, cloves and ginger and pour it into the butter mixture. Stir until almost blended, but don't overmix. Wrap tightly and refrigerate for 30 to 60 minutes or until firm.

Preheat your oven to 350°F (177°C) and line several baking sheets with parchment paper.

To make the cookie coating, in a small, shallow bowl, whisk together the granulated sugar, cinnamon, nutmeg, cloves and ginger. Once the dough is chilled, gently roll 1½ tablespoons (21 g) of dough between your palms into a ball. Give the dough ball a generous coating of the sugar-spice mixture and set on the baking sheet, leaving 2 inches (5 cm) of space between balls. Bake one sheet at a time in the center of the oven for 10 to 11 minutes. Let them cool on the baking sheet for 10 minutes and then move to a rack to finish cooling.

To make the frosting, while the cookies cool, mix together the butter, cream cheese, sugar, cinnamon and nutmeg until smooth. Add 1 tablespoon (15 ml) of milk to thin, adding more if necessary to get the desired consistency. Smear a generous dollop over the tops of the cookies.

CHOCOLATE PUMPKIN SWIRL COOKIES

Chocolate and pumpkin are such a natural flavor combination, but they are tricky to throw together. The usual spices paired with pumpkin can compete with chocolate for flavor domination. In these, I heavily spiced the pumpkin part of the cookie and then entrenched the chocolate part with bits of more chocolate. The only difficult part of making these is remembering not to add all of the flour at once. If you make it past that point, they're a piece of cake.

MAKES 63 COOKIES

8 tablespoons (115 g) unsalted butter, room temperature

1 cup (210 g) light brown sugar, packed

½ cup (96 g) granulated sugar

½ cup (118 ml) sunflower seed oil or other neutral oil

½ cup (118 ml) pure pumpkin puree (not pumpkin pie filling)

2 large eggs, room temperature

1 tablespoon (15 ml) real vanilla extract

2⅓ cups plus ¼ cup (351 g) all-purpose flour, divided

1½ teaspoons (7 g) sea salt

1 teaspoon baking powder

1 teaspoon baking soda

2 teaspoons (5 g) cinnamon

½ teaspoon nutmeg

½ teaspoon cloves

½ teaspoon ginger

½ teaspoon allspice

¼ cup (21 g) unsweetened dark (Dutch process) cocoa powder

1¼ cups (150 g) dark chocolate, coarsely chopped

Sea salt flakes to garnish, optional

In an electric stand mixer fitted with the paddle attachment, mix the butter with the brown sugar and granulated sugar on medium for 4 minutes or until smooth and creamy. Blend in the oil and pumpkin puree. Add in the eggs, one at a time, taking care that each is well blended before adding in the next. Add in the vanilla and continue to mix on medium for 1 to 2 minutes, or until everything is well incorporated, taking care to scrape down the sides and bottom of the bowl.

In another medium bowl, whisk together the 2⅓ cups (317 g) of all-purpose flour, salt, baking powder and baking soda. Add the flour mixture to the pumpkin mixture and mix until barely combined.

Evenly divide the dough between two bowls. To one bowl add the remaining ¼ cup (34 g) of flour, cinnamon, nutmeg, cloves, ginger and allspice. To the other add the cocoa powder and the chocolate chunks.

Wrap the dough separately in plastic wrap and stash in the fridge for 45 minutes to firm up a bit if the dough is too sticky.

Preheat your oven to 350°F (177°C). Cover several baking sheets with parchment paper.

Grab 1 teaspoon of the chocolate dough and 1 teaspoon of the pumpkin dough and press them together into a small ball. Repeat, adding 1 more teaspoon of each to the dough ball. Gently roll the dough between the palms of your hands until it gets all swirly. Set the dough balls on a baking sheet 2 inches (5 cm) apart. Sprinkle with sea salt flakes, if using.

Bake one sheet at a time in the center of the oven for 9 minutes. They will appear slightly underdone.

Let them cool for about 5 minutes on the baking sheet and then transfer to the cooling rack.

DARK RYE MIDNIGHT COOKIES

Put on your smoking jacket and bust out the brown liquor...we're making that kinda cookie. I absolutely love pairing rye with chocolate because it really tempers anything cloying and brings out the true essence of chocolate without the sometimes-overt sugariness. And bourbon-soaked cherries are never a bad idea. Ever. Soak them as long as possible. These cookies were also tested with teff, white whole-wheat flour and bread flour. All of the flours worked (in case you're in a pinch), but the dark rye and teff were my favorites for the complexities that they added to the cookie.

MAKES 36 COOKIES

3 cups (420 g) dried tart cherries

½ cup (118 ml) good quality bourbon

12 tablespoons (172 g) unsalted butter

1½ cups plus 1¾ cups (390 g) dark chocolate, coarsely chopped, divided

1¼ cups (240 g) granulated sugar

3 large eggs, room temperature

1 large egg white, room temperature

1 tablespoon (15 ml) real vanilla extract

2 cups (204 g) dark rye flour

1 cup (84 g) unsweetened dark (Dutch processed) cocoa powder

1½ teaspoons (7 g) sea salt

1½ teaspoons (6 g) baking powder

1 teaspoon baking soda

Smoked sea salt flakes or regular sea salt flakes, optional

In a small bowl, combine the cherries and bourbon. Cover and set aside for several hours or refrigerate up to several days. Stir periodically.

In a medium, heat-safe bowl, add the butter, 1½ cups (180 g) of chocolate and the granulated sugar and set over a medium saucepan of simmering water. Do not let the bowl touch the water or let the water come to a boil. Stir frequently until melted and almost smooth. Place a towel on the counter and set the bowl on top of it and stir out any remaining lumps. Whisk in the eggs and egg white, one at a time, making sure each is well blended before adding in the next. Stir in the vanilla until combined.

In a medium bowl, whisk together the dark rye flour, cocoa powder, sea salt, baking powder and baking soda. Add this to the butter mixture and stir until just combined. Fold in the bourbon-soaked cherries (discard any remaining liquid or make a cocktail with it) and the 1¾ cups (210 g) of chocolate until evenly distributed, taking care not to over mix the dough. Cover the dough tightly and refrigerate for at least 20 minutes, or until firm and some of the stickiness is gone. If using a cookie scoop or spoons, feel free to use the dough straight away otherwise it will be too sticky to handle.

Preheat the oven to 350°F (177°C) and cover several baking sheets with parchment paper. Roll 2 tablespoons (28 g) of dough into a ball and place 2 inches (5 cm) apart from each other on the prepared baking sheet. Wet your hands (so they're damp, not dripping wet) and press the balls down so they form little discs. Sprinkle each with a pinch of sea salt flakes, if using.

Bake one sheet at a time in the center of the oven for 10 minutes. Let the cookies cool for 5 to 10 minutes on the baking sheet, and then transfer to racks to finish cooling.

> **TIP**
> Only use a bourbon that you would enjoy sipping. And if you would prefer to abstain from booze, feel free to soak the cherries in water for a spell to plump them up.

HAZELNUT MINT CHIP COOLERS

These are similar to Mexican wedding cookies, Italian wedding cookies and snowball cookies. I don't like crispy or crumbly cookies, but these are both and I love it. And everyone I feed them to loves them. They're fresh and chocolatey and crumbly and melt-in-your-mouth deliciousness. I wanted flavors that hinted of mint chip ice cream...so we throw the chips in the processor at the last minute so we still have some small chunks hanging around. If you don't have a food processor you could chop everything up by hand, but then you may hate me.

MAKES 30 COOKIES

2 cups (264 g) raw unskinned hazelnuts

1¾ cups (239 g) all-purpose flour

¼ cup (21 g) unsweetened dark (Dutch process) cocoa powder

⅓ cup (64 g) granulated sugar

1 teaspoon baking powder

¾ teaspoon sea salt

16 tablespoons (230 g) unsalted butter, cut into 16 pieces, room temperature

2 teaspoons (10 ml) peppermint extract

1¼ cups (150 g) dark or semisweet chocolate chips

1½ cups (195 g) powdered sugar

Place the hazelnuts in a large, heavy-bottomed skillet over medium heat, frequently stirring for 5 minutes or until fragrant and the skins are slightly darkened. Set aside and cool completely.

Cover several baking sheets with parchment paper.

Place the cooled hazelnuts in a food processor fitted with the blade attachment and pulse until finely chopped. Add in the flour, cocoa powder, granulated sugar, baking powder and sea salt, and pulse 10 times to combine. Sprinkle the butter and peppermint extract over the top and run the machine for 30 to 60 seconds. Add in the chocolate chips and pulse until combined and a ball forms. Make sure the moisture is evenly distributed throughout the dough.

Gently roll 1½ tablespoons (21 g) of dough into a ball and place on the prepared baking sheet leaving 1 inch (2.5 cm) between each ball. Freeze for 20 minutes or refrigerate for 40 minutes.

Heat the oven to 325°F (163°C). Bake one sheet at a time for 20 minutes in the center of the oven. Let the cookies cool on the sheet for 10 minutes.

Place the powdered sugar in a medium shallow bowl. With the cookies still warm, coat them in the powdered sugar. They will be fragile, so take care to dust the sugar over the cookies rather than rolling the cookie in the sugar. Place them back on the baking sheet to cool for an hour. Once cool, coat with one final dusting of powdered sugar for a nice thick coat.

THE ULTIMATE
HOLIDAY COOKIE
EXCHANGE

There is something about late fall into early winter that makes me want to bake like a maniac. I want my house to smell like spiced cider, mistletoe hanging from every doorway and all kinds of cookies nestled in jars and displayed like the queens they are in lidded pedestals. If there is ever a time of year to show your love through food, this is it. This is your season. So, I'm going to need you to get extra cozy, throw some evergreen about, soundtrack some vintage holiday tunes in the background (the kind that's begging for a martini companion) and start bringing your butter and eggs to room temperature.

Some cookies I'm really excited to share include the Spiced Brown Butter Muscovado Sugar Cookies (page 111). These cookies are everything familiar with the spices and maple glaze and totally unexpected in the flavors that only dark muscovado sugar can bring to the table. If you're short on time but still want to deliver some holiday magic, I'd like to direct you towards the 24k Gold Hazelnut Bars (page 107), which are gorgeous and come together in the blink of an eye. If you want a baking project you can really sink your teeth into, something to while away the day while the snow falls outside, I'd like you to try Peppermint Candy Macarons (page 127) (but not if it's humid), Mexican Hot Chocolate S'more Cookies (page 108) or Spiced Gingerbread Cookies Two Ways (page 125).

If I were going to throw a holiday cookie exchange, I would want everyone to bring these cookies. This chapter should feel like snowflakes, evergreen, Dean Martin and cheer. And if you're not happy after reading it, I don't know if we can be friends. It's that simple.

Shall we holiday?

DARK CHOCOLATE FIVE-SPICE TRUFFLES

Five-spice powder is one of my favorite spice blends to use around the holiday season. The combination of cinnamon, cloves, star anise, Szechuan peppercorns and fennel seeds pairs perfectly with cranberries and, more to the point, chocolate! These come together quickly, and the only inconvenience is having to wait for them to firm up enough to scoop. This is one of those recipes that I highly recommend using a 1-tablespoon (15-ml) cookie scoop for. They'll make pretty close-to-perfect, truffle-like mounds. I topped each truffle with some dried marigold, because gold and the holidays are the perfect companions, don't you think? Feel free to get frisky and top them with cacao nibs, chopped hazelnuts, dried rose petals or whatever might strike your fancy.

MAKES 40 TRUFFLES

1½ cups (180 g) bittersweet chocolate, finely chopped

⅓ cup (79 ml) heavy whipping cream, warm

3 tablespoons (43 g) unsalted butter, room temperature

½ teaspoon five-spice powder

TRUFFLE COATING

2½ cups (300 g) dark chocolate, finely chopped

2 tablespoons (3 g) dried marigold flowers, to garnish

Place the chocolate in a heat-safe bowl, pour the warm cream over and add the butter. Cover with plastic wrap and set aside for 5 minutes. Uncover and stir until smooth and glossy. Stir in the five-spice powder. Pour into an 8 x 11-inch (20.3 x 28–cm) casserole dish and cover with plastic wrap. Set in the fridge but check frequently (I like to check every 30 minutes) and don't let it get too firm. Beyond 1½ hours it will become too hard to scoop.

Cover a baking sheet with parchment paper. Using a cookie scoop, scrape up 1 tablespoon (14 g) of chocolate. Scrape the bottom of the scoop against the side of the dish so that it's flat and release the truffle onto the prepared baking sheet. Place the truffles in the freezer for several hours.

For the truffle coating, in a medium, heat-safe bowl, add the chocolate and set over a medium saucepan of simmering water. Do not let the bowl touch the water or let the water come to a boil. Stir frequently until barely melted and not quite smooth. Set on top of a hand towel and stir until all of the lumps are gone. Set aside, stirring frequently while it cools.

Set some parchment paper underneath a cooling rack.

Using a dipping or regular fork, dip the frozen truffles into the chocolate coating. Tap the fork on the side of the bowl, letting the excess chocolate fall back into the bowl. Place the truffle on the cooling rack and immediately garnish with dried marigold flowers, if using. Let the truffles set for 1 hour before transferring to an airtight container (lined in parchment with parchment separating each layer of truffles) to store in the fridge until ready to serve for up to several weeks.

24K GOLD HAZELNUT BARS

Ladies and gentlemen, an easy peasy recipe that dazzles and brings a little bling to your holiday gatherings. These bars take no more than several minutes on the stovetop (you heard me, SEVERAL MINUTES), and then we walk away, put our feet up and sip some spiked eggnog while they cool. Smear some melted white chocolate over the cooled top, sprinkle with more hazelnuts and then sparingly apply some edible 24K gold, letting our inner baller fly. This, my friends, wins the MVP award for easiest holiday treat EVER.

MAKES 15 BAR COOKIES

1 (14-ounce [392-ml]) can sweetened condensed milk

2½ cups (300 g) dark chocolate, finely chopped

2 tablespoons (14 g) unsweetened dark (Dutch processed) cocoa powder

2 tablespoons (29 g) unsalted butter

4 tablespoons (60 ml) Frangelico

1 teaspoon real vanilla extract

½ teaspoon sea salt

1½ cups (202 g) raw hazelnuts, coarsely chopped, divided

1¼ cups (150 g) white chocolate, finely chopped

1 tablespoon (14 g) vegetable shortening

1 sheet edible gold leaf

Grease and line a 9 x 9–inch (23 x 23–cm) baking dish with parchment paper, letting the excess hang over the sides. Set aside.

Add the sweetened condensed milk, dark chocolate, cocoa powder and butter to a medium heavy-bottomed saucepan and stir over medium-low heat until smooth and melted. This should take several minutes. Add in the Frangelico, vanilla, sea salt and 1 cup (132 g) of hazelnuts, stirring to combine. Pour the mixture into the prepared pan, smoothing the top with an offset spatula or the back of a spoon. Let set for several hours.

In a medium, heat-safe bowl, place the white chocolate and shortening and set over a medium saucepan over simmering water. Don't let the water touch the bowl or let the water come to a boil. Stir constantly until melted. Pour the white chocolate evenly over the top of the chocolate, again smoothing with a clean offset spatula or the back of a spoon. Sprinkle the remaining hazelnuts along the edges, leaving the middle part free from nuts. Let set for an hour.

Grab a clean, new paint brush, a glass of water and your edible gold leaf. Press the gold leaf around the surface of the white chocolate, leaving little bits of gold leaf, and then dampen your brush and lightly brush it over the gold leaf to spread it around. Use sparingly, we're going for vintage vibes, not Miami after dark.

Use the overhanging parchment paper to pull the bars out of the baking dish and cut with a sharp knife, cleaning in between cuts for nice, clean bars. In the summer I keep these in the fridge until serving and in the cooler months I let them hang on the counter. Either way, make sure they're wrapped tightly if not eating immediately.

MEXICAN HOT CHOCOLATE S'MORE COOKIES

I have memories of lounging by my Aunt Kathy's pool in the summers shoving marshmallow cookies in my mouth by the dozens. Ahh the metabolism of youth. For the cookies, I really spiced up the graham-like crust for holiday vibes and topped it with a classic marshmallow. The chocolate drizzle over the top has some cinnamon and a hit of cayenne, which could be easily omitted if a little spice wrinkles your feathers. None of these steps are particularly difficult, but when you come to the marshmallow part make sure you prep everything in advance as you'll want to move fast before the marshmallow sets.

MAKES ABOUT 50 COOKIES

⅓ cup (73 g) light brown sugar, packed

¼ cup (60 ml) unsulphured molasses

¼ cup (59 ml) sunflower seed oil or other neutral oil

¼ cup (60 ml) milk

1 tablespoon (15 ml) real vanilla extract

1 cup (120 g) white whole-wheat flour

1 cup (136 g) all-purpose flour

1 teaspoon cinnamon

1 teaspoon baking powder

1 teaspoon baking soda

¾ teaspoon sea salt

MARSHMALLOWS

½ cup (65 g) powdered sugar

½ cup (76 g) cornstarch

2½ packages (18 g) unflavored gelatin

1½ cups (288 g) granulated sugar

1 cup (237 ml) corn syrup

¼ teaspoon salt

1 tablespoon (17 g) vanilla bean paste or 1 vanilla bean split and scraped

To make the cookies, in a medium bowl whisk together the sugar, molasses, oil, milk and vanilla.

In another medium bowl, whisk together the whole-wheat flour, all-purpose flour, cinnamon, baking powder, baking soda and salt. Add to the sugar mixture and stir until just combined. Wrap tightly and place in the fridge for 30 to 60 minutes.

Cover several baking sheets with parchment paper and set aside. Dust another piece of parchment with flour and, if you have a silicone baking mat, place it beneath the parchment to keep it from moving around the countertop while you roll the dough. Roll the dough to ½-inch (1.3-cm) thickness between the two sheets of parchment paper. Lightly dust the top of the dough with flour and cut out as many 1¼-inch (3.3-cm) circles as possible. Place the circles on the prepared baking sheet about 1 inch (2.5 cm) apart from one another. Roll out any excess dough and repeat until all of the dough is used up. Try to get as many circles on the first go—if you re-roll the dough more than once, you run the risk of getting a tough cookie. Place the cookies in the freezer for 15 minutes or the fridge for 30 minutes.

Preheat your oven to 350°F (177°C).

Bake one sheet at a time in the center of the oven for 9 minutes. Remove the cookies from the baking sheet and let them finish cooling on a rack.

To make the marshmallows, in a small bowl whisk the powdered sugar and cornstarch and sift some of the mixture to cover the bottom of a baking sheet. Reserve the remaining mixture to sift over the finished marshmallows. Fit two pastry bags with round tips. Spray the insides of the bags with nonstick spray. This will keep your marshmallows from sticking to the bag. Set aside.

Place the gelatin in an electric stand mixer fitted with the whisk attachment and add ¾ cup (180 ml) of cold water. Let sit until the gelatin has bloomed and the water looks cloudy and gelatinous.

(continued)

CHOCOLATE COATING

2¾ cups (330 g) dark chocolate, coarsely chopped

2 tablespoons (28 g) vegetable shortening

1 teaspoon real vanilla extract

¾ teaspoon cinnamon

⅛ to ¼ teaspoon cayenne (depending on how much heat you want)

In a medium heavy-bottomed saucepan, add the granulated sugar, corn syrup, salt and ½ cup (118 ml) of water, and stir over medium heat until the sugar dissolves. Then turn up the heat to high and cook until the mixture registers between 230 to 240°F (110 to 115°C) on a candy thermometer then remove from the heat.

Turn the mixer on low and slowly add in the hot sugar mixture. Turn the mixer on high and whisk for about 7 to 10 minutes, or until the mixture is thick, fluffy and barely warm. Add in the vanilla and run the mixer until it's distributed evenly throughout. Scoop the mixture into the prepared pastry bags and pipe your marshmallows into kisses (think of a chocolate kiss, same shape) on the prepared baking sheet. You want the base of the marshmallow to be about the same size as or smaller than the size of your cookies. Hold the pastry bag perpendicular and slightly above the baking sheet and push out some marshmallow into a circle the size of a quarter, pausing for 1 second before pulling the tip straight up to make a nice tip at the top. Repeat with the remaining marshmallow. These will get easier the more you do. Sprinkle the marshmallows with the remaining sugar-cornstarch mixture and let the marshmallows sit at room temperature for several hours and up to overnight.

Once the marshmallows are set, gently roll them in the powdered sugar on the baking sheet to get them completely covered, so that they aren't sticky and are easy to handle. Brush off any excess powdered sugar.

To assemble, set a cooling rack over a baking sheet covered with parchment paper.

To make the chocolate coating, in a medium, heat-safe bowl add the chocolate, shortening, vanilla, cinnamon and cayenne and set over a medium saucepan of simmering water. Do not let the bowl touch the water or let the water come to a boil. Stir frequently until barely melted and not quite smooth. Set on top of a hand towel and stir until all of the lumps are gone. Set aside, stirring frequently while it cools.

Set the cookies on the cooling rack and dip the marshmallows in the chocolate coating completely. Use a chocolate dipping fork or regular fork to do this. Hold the marshmallow over the bowl, letting the excess chocolate fall back into the bowl, and then set on top of a cookie. Repeat with the remaining marshmallows and let them sit until the chocolate is fully hardened, about 1 hour. If at any point the chocolate gets too thick to dip the marshmallows, simply place it back over the simmering water and stir until it loosens up a bit.

You may end up with extra marshmallows, in which case marshmallow kisses in hot chocolate are never a bad idea.

SPICED BROWN BUTTER
MUSCOVADO SUGAR COOKIES

I am head-over-heels excited to share this one with you because I've frankly never tasted anything like it, and that's a good thing. I was completely inspired by the look of the stamped molasses cookies in the cookbook *Sweet*. I wanted to create a cookie with a wee different flavor profile and utilize cookie stamps, which are so pretty and gorgeous that I think we all need cookie stamps in our baking arsenal. Picture a sugar cookie made with brown butter and caramel-esque muscovado and loaded with holiday spices. We roll it out thick, stamp it like a boss and then drizzle with the simplest spiced maple glaze. The key to not losing the details of the stamp is giving this cookie ample freezer time and gently brushing off excess glaze.

MAKES 24 COOKIES

24 tablespoons (344 g) unsalted butter

1 cup (210 g) dark muscovado sugar, packed

½ cup (96 g) granulated sugar

2 large eggs, room temperature

1 tablespoon (15 ml) real vanilla extract

3 cups (408 g) all-purpose flour

1 cup (136 g) bread flour

2 teaspoons (5 g) cinnamon

1 teaspoon allspice

1 teaspoon cloves

1 teaspoon ginger

1 teaspoon sea salt

½ teaspoon cardamom

To make the cookies, place the butter in a medium heavy-bottomed saucepan and melt over medium heat. Once melted, crank up the heat to medium high, stirring constantly. Small golden bits will start to settle on the bottom of the pan, and it will start to have a nutty aroma. This should take around 3 to 5 minutes. Once this happens, take the pan off of the heat and pour the butter into the bowl of an electric stand mixer fitted with the paddle attachment. Once cooled slightly, add the muscovado and granulated sugar and mix on medium until blended. The mixture will be thick. Add in the eggs, one at a time, making sure to blend completely before adding in the next. Add in the vanilla and mix for 1 minute more. Be sure to break up any large muscovado lumps.

In a large bowl, whisk together the all-purpose flour, bread flour, cinnamon, allspice, cloves, ginger, sea salt and cardamom. Add this to the brown butter mixture and mix on low until the mixture comes together and is no longer crumbs. Separate into two equal halves and pat each mound of dough into a disc. Typically sugar cookie dough needs a light hand. Not this dough. You'll need to almost knead it to get it to adhere together. Press any cracks or fissures together.

Place a dough disc between two layers of parchment paper. If you have a silicone baking mat, place it underneath the parchment to keep it from sliding on the counter. Roll the dough to ½-inch (1.3-cm) thickness. Pull the dough with the parchment onto a baking sheet and chill in the freezer for 5 to 10 minutes or in the fridge for 10 to 20 minutes, max. The dough should chill quickly. If at any point the dough starts sticking to the floured cookie stamps, put it back in the freezer for 5 minutes or in the fridge for 10 minutes. Conversely, if it's too chilled, let it come closer to room temperature to stamp, or it will be too hard.

(continued)

MAPLE GLAZE

2 cups (260 g) powdered sugar

1 tablespoon (15 ml) real maple syrup

½ teaspoon maple extract, optional

4 tablespoons (60 ml) milk, or more to thin

Cover several baking sheets with parchment paper.

If using cookie stamps, dip the cookie stamps in some flour and dust off the excess. Evenly press the cookie stamp onto the dough, making sure to press firmly to get the detailed imprint, and then use a fluted, round cutter to cut the cookie from the dough. Grab a spatula to move the cut-out cookie to your prepared baking sheets. Repeat with the remaining cookies.

Preheat the oven to 375°F (190°C) and make sure a rack is in the top third of the oven at least 6 inches (15 cm) from the heat source.

Place the cookies in the freezer for 30 minutes and then take them directly from the freezer to the top rack of the oven and bake for 9 minutes. It's crucial not to overbake these. Let the cookies cool for 5 minutes on the baking sheet and then transfer to a rack to finish cooling.

To make the glaze, in a small bowl, whisk together the powdered sugar, maple syrup, maple extract, if using, and milk until you have a thin glaze. Place a baking sheet underneath the cooling rack. Dip the cooled cookies into the glaze, letting the excess drip back into the bowl...you want the glaze to be thin enough that you can see the detail from the cookie stamps. Set the cookies back on the cooling rack to dry completely and serve!

TIP

I used a 2½-inch (6.3-cm) cookie stamp for these. If you don't have any cookie stamps, these are definitely still worth making using just a round cookie cutter.

TAI TAI'S PEPPERMINT SANDWICH COOKIE

This is one of those cookies that I've been making for friends since I lived in China. Two chocolatey, chewy cookies sandwich a hefty dollop of peppermint cream that is heavily laced with crushed peppermint candies for added crunch. If these don't put a little holiday spirit in your step, I don't know what will. I've often wondered if this peppermint cream would make a nice winter salve to soothe my December skin?

MAKES ABOUT 20 COOKIE SANDWICHES

1¾ cups (210 g) semisweet chocolate, coarsely chopped

½ cup (118 ml) sunflower seed oil or other neutral oil

3 large eggs, room temperature

¾ cup (158) light brown sugar, packed

¾ cup (144 g) granulated sugar

2 teaspoons (11 ml) pure vanilla extract

1 cup (136 g) bread flour

¾ cup (103 g) all-purpose flour

¼ cup (21 g) unsweetened cocoa powder

1½ teaspoons (7 g) sea salt

1 teaspoon baking powder

1 teaspoon baking soda

1½ cups (270 g) dark or semisweet chocolate chips

PEPPERMINT CREAM

½ cup (115 g) unsalted butter, room temperature

½ cup (115 g) vegetable shortening

3½ cups (455 g) powdered sugar

2 teaspoons (10 ml) peppermint extract

3 tablespoons (45 ml) milk

½ cup (116 g) finely crushed peppermint candies (about 8 medium-sized candy canes)

To make the cookie, melt the semisweet chocolate and oil in the microwave in a large microwave-safe bowl or in a double boiler. I usually do 1 minute on high, but microwaves are funky so keep an eye on things. Stir the chocolate to get rid of any chunks. Sometimes it will look chunky, but if you give it 20 or so stirs, you'll get rid of all of the chunks without overheating it. Let the chocolate cool slightly and then whisk in your eggs, brown sugar, granulated sugar and vanilla extract.

In another bowl, whisk together the bread flour, all-purpose flour, cocoa powder, sea salt, baking powder and baking soda. Pour this into the chocolate mixture and stir until the dough is just starting to come together. Add the chocolate chips and mix until just barely combined. Wrap tightly and chill for 30 minutes in the fridge.

Preheat your oven to 350°F (177°C) and line several baking sheets with parchment paper.

Gently roll 1 tablespoon (14 g) of dough into a ball and place on the cookie sheet, allowing about 1 inch (2.5 cm) between each dough ball. Try to make the dough balls as spherical as possible and equal in size so they will pair up nicely when smooshing the peppermint cream between them.

Bake one sheet at a time for 8 minutes in the center of the oven. You want to slightly undercook these. Allow the cookies to cool on the sheet for 5 to 10 minutes, then transfer to a cooling rack.

To make the cream, while the cookies are cooling, place the butter and shortening in an electric stand mixer fitted with the paddle attachment. Mix on medium-low until well blended. Add in the powdered sugar, peppermint extract and milk and continue blending until nice and creamy. Lastly, add in the crushed peppermint candy and mix until evenly distributed throughout the cream.

Pair up cookies that are of equal size, give a generous (I mean it) smear of peppermint cream on one side and smash another cookie on top. If you want it to look nice and tidy, run a finger around the outside of the cream to smooth it out.

WHITE CHOCOLATE FUDGE BROWNIES

The holidays are such a CRAZY busy time, and I feel like I'm constantly making something to take to a party or for Gavin and Stella to take to school. These come together quickly, use basic ingredients and feel super festive with the drizzle of white chocolate that's dotted with bright, fresh cranberries and raw, green pistachios. My one caution: do not use frozen cranberries or your chocolate will seize while you're trying to get all artsy with the top. Other than that, these babies are a breeze.

MAKES 15 BROWNIES

1¼ cups (150 g) dark chocolate, finely chopped

1 cup (192 g) granulated sugar

¾ cup (158 g) light brown sugar, packed

8 tablespoons (115 g) unsalted butter, cut into 8 pieces, room temperature

⅓ cup (79 ml) sunflower seed oil or other neutral oil

4 large eggs, room temperature

1 tablespoon (15 ml) freshly brewed espresso or strong coffee

1 tablespoon (15 ml) real vanilla extract

1 cup (125 g) all-purpose flour

⅔ cup (74 g) unsweetened dark (Dutch process) cocoa powder

1 teaspoon sea salt

2⅓ cups (232 g) fresh cranberries, divided

¾ cup (90 g) white chocolate, melted

2 tablespoons (20 g) raw pistachios, shelled and coarsely chopped

2 teaspoons (10 g) sea salt flakes, optional

Preheat the oven to 350°F (177°C). Grease an 8 x 11–inch (20.3 x 28–cm) baking dish and line with parchment paper, letting the excess fall over the sides.

Place the chocolate, granulated sugar, brown sugar, butter and oil in a double boiler over medium-low heat, stirring frequently until melted. Place a towel on the counter and set the bowl on top of it. Whisk in the eggs, one at a time, making sure each is well blended before adding in the next. Add in the espresso and vanilla and stir until well blended.

In a small bowl, whisk together the flour, cocoa powder and salt. Add this to the chocolate mixture and stir until just combined. Fold in 2 cups (199 g) of cranberries.

Pour the batter into the prepared baking dish. Use the back of your spoon to even the top a bit. Drizzle the melted white chocolate over the top and drag a knife through the batter to swirl the white chocolate in a pretty design. Sprinkle with the pistachios and the remaining ⅓ cup (33 g) of cranberries. If using the sea salt flakes, add them now.

Bake on the middle rack of the oven for 25 minutes. When done, they will have a bit of jiggle in the middle, and if you test with a toothpick a wee bit of batter will coat it. This is a good thing.

Let cool in the pan for several hours, and if you want super uber fudgy brownies shove them in the fridge for several hours before serving.

When it's time to cut the brownies, use a very sharp knife, cut straight up and down and use a wet paper towel to clean off the knife in between cuts.

PEPPERMINT BARK SHORTBREAD BITES

I just knew I needed something with peppermint bark in here, but I didn't want to do actual peppermint bark. There were several underwhelming iterations before landing on these lovelies. The chocolate shortbread is equal parts buttery and sandy in all the best ways. And chocolate and peppermint? It just never gets old. The sprinkling of peppermint around the perimeter makes these look like holiday wreaths. I think. You decide.

MAKES 24 COOKIES

20 tablespoons (287 g) unsalted butter, cut into 20 pieces, room temperature

¾ cup (158 g) light brown sugar, packed

1 large egg yolk, room temperature

1 teaspoon real vanilla extract

¼ teaspoon peppermint extract

2 cups (272 g) all-purpose flour

¼ cup (21 g) unsweetened dark (Dutch process) cocoa powder

½ teaspoon sea salt

½ teaspoon baking powder

½ cup (96 g) sparkling sugar

COOKIE COATING

1⅓ cups (160 g) dark chocolate, coarsely chopped

¾ cup (90 g) white chocolate, coarsely chopped

⅓ cup (77 g) peppermint candy, finely crushed and divided

To make the cookies, in an electric stand mixer fitted with the paddle attachment, add the butter and brown sugar and mix on medium for about 4 minutes, or until well blended. With the mixer on low, add in the egg yolk, vanilla and peppermint extract and run for 2 minutes more or until completely blended. Scrape down the sides and bottom of the bowl to make sure everything is well incorporated.

In a medium bowl, whisk together the flour, cocoa powder, salt and baking powder. Add this to the butter mixture and run on low for 2 minutes, or until everything is combined and the dough has come together. Separate the dough into two hunks and shape each into a log with about a 2-inch (5-cm) circumference. It's a little messy, but you can do it. Grab two pieces of plastic wrap, place a dough log on each, wrap tightly and roll the logs on the counter to round them out a bit. Place in the freezer for 1 hour or until firm.

Preheat the oven to 350°F (177°C) and cover several baking sheets with parchment paper. Place the sparkling sugar in a pie plate or casserole dish. Set aside.

Once the logs are firm and chilled, roll them in the sparkling sugar to coat and then cut ½-inch (1.3-cm) thick slices using a sharp knife. Place them on the baking sheets, leaving 2 inches (5 cm) between cookies. Place the cookies in the freezer for 10 minutes or the fridge for 20 minutes.

Bake one sheet at a time in center of the oven for 14 minutes. Let them cool on the baking sheet for 10 minutes and then transfer to a rack to finish cooling.

To make the cookie coating, in a medium, heat-safe bowl add the dark chocolate and set over a medium saucepan of simmering water. Do not let the bowl touch the water. Stir frequently until melted and smooth and then turn off the heat. In another medium, heat-safe bowl add the white chocolate and set over a medium saucepan of simmering water. Do not let the bowl touch the water. Do not let the water come to a boil. Stir frequently until melted and smooth and then turn off the heat.

Dip the tops of the cookies in the dark chocolate, letting the excess chocolate run back into the bowl. Drop some drops of white chocolate over the top and use a toothpick to swirl white chocolate circles into the dark chocolate. Sprinkle the outer edges of the cookies with the crushed peppermint candy. Let the chocolate set before serving or storing.

CRÈME FRÂICHE CRANBERRY PECAN PIE BITES

I hate to sound cranky but I can't stand the word Tassie. Which is what these actually are, but we're calling them pie bites because that's what they should be called. And this crust. Don't even get me started. It's the easiest thing to throw together and is flaky and tart and fresh and the perfect capsule to hold this pecan-cranberry filling that is teeming with caramelized brown sugar and orange flavors. These are super easy and super delicious and you have to make them right now.

MAKES 24 COOKIES

8 tablespoons (115 g) unsalted butter, cut into 8 pieces, room temperature

7½ ounces (213 g) crème frâiche, room temperature

1 tablespoon (9 g) orange zest

½ teaspoon sea salt

1¾ cups (238 g) all-purpose flour

PIE FILLING

1 cup (210 g) light or dark brown sugar, packed

1 large egg, room temperature

1 tablespoon (14 g) unsalted butter, melted

1 tablespoon (9 g) orange zest

1 teaspoon real vanilla extract

¼ teaspoon sea salt

48 fresh cranberries

⅓ cup (40 g) pecans, toasted and coarsely chopped

¼ cup (33 g) powdered sugar, to garnish

To make the crust, in a medium bowl add the butter, crème frâiche, orange zest and salt and and mash with the back of a fork until well combined. Sprinkle the flour over the top and use a pastry blender, two forks or your hands to combine the flour into the butter-crème frâiche mixture. Make sure there aren't any dry flour patches remaining. The texture may seem a little strange but trust me. Wrap tightly and stash in the fridge for several hours until firm, or up to overnight.

Preheat the oven to 350°F (177°C) and grease a mini-muffin tin with 24 muffin wells.

On a floured surface roll the dough to ¼-inch (¾-cm) thickness. Use a 2¼-inch (5.7-cm) round cutter and cut 24 circles out of the dough. Press the dough circles into the muffin tin, gently pressing so they lay flat on the bottom of each well. Set in the fridge to chill while you prepare the rest of the ingredients.

To make the filling, in a medium bowl whisk together the brown sugar, egg, melted butter, orange zest, vanilla and salt until combined, and set aside.

To assemble, distribute the pecans evenly among the crusts. Add two cranberries to each muffin well. Put 1 to 2 teaspoons (5 to 10 g) of filling in with the pecans and cranberries, so that it just reaches the top of the mini crusts.

Bake in the center of the oven for 30 to 35 minutes, or until puffed and baked through. Let them cool for 5 minutes in the muffin tin and then turn out onto a rack to finish cooling. Use a knife to loosen any petite pies that resist coming out.

Once cool, sift the powdered sugar over the tops and serve.

BLOOD ORANGE JAMMY SAMMIES

Blood oranges are one of the many citrus wonders of winter. You will want to make this jam just to smear on toast in the morning, I promise. Feel free to use a different size or style cookie cutter and also to sub in different citrus at other times of the year when blood oranges aren't easily found.

MAKES 30 SAMMIES

ORANGE JAM

1 pound (454 g) whole blood oranges, peeled, coarsely chopped (about 3 blood oranges)

2 tablespoons (19 g) blood orange zest

1 lemon, juiced and zested

¾ cup (177 ml) water

1 cup (192 g) granulated sugar

1 cinnamon stick

1 star anise

1 clove

SANDWICH COOKIE

24 tablespoons (344 g) unsalted butter, cut into 24 pieces, room temperature

1½ cups (288 g) granulated sugar

2 large eggs, room temperature

1 tablespoon (9 g) blood orange zest

¾ teaspoon pure vanilla extract

¼ teaspoon almond extract

3 cups (408 g) bread flour

1 cup (136 g) all-purpose flour

1 teaspoon sea salt

½ teaspoon baking powder

½ teaspoon baking soda

To make the jam, add the chopped blood orange, blood orange zest, lemon juice, lemon zest, water, granulated sugar, cinnamon, star anise and clove to a medium saucepan and bring to a boil. Continue at a rolling boil for about 35 minutes, or until the mixture has darkened a bit and thickened. Let cool and then put in the fridge until ready to assemble the cookies. The jam will continue to thicken as it cools.

To make the cookies, in an electric stand mixer fitted with the paddle attachment, mix the butter and sugar on medium until light and fluffy. Add in the eggs, one at a time, scraping down the sides and bottom of the bowl and making sure each is fully blended before adding the next. Add in the blood orange zest, vanilla and almond extract and mix for 1 minute more to fully blend.

In a large bowl, whisk together the bread flour, all-purpose flour, sea salt, baking powder and baking soda. Add to the butter mixture and mix on low until just blended. Separate into two equal halves and pat each mound of dough into a disc. Wrap tightly in plastic wrap and stash in the fridge for 30 to 60 minutes to rest. Don't chill for longer, or it will be too difficult to roll out. If this happens, let the dough come close to room temperature before attempting to roll out. You want it soft enough so that it rolls out without cracking, but cool enough that it's not too sticky.

Preheat the oven to 350°F (177°C) and cover several baking sheets in parchment paper. Let the dough sit for 10 minutes or longer to soften when removing from the fridge and place it between two lightly floured layers of parchment paper. If you have a silicone baking mat, place it underneath the parchment to keep it from sliding on the counter. Roll the dough to ¼-inch (0.7-cm) thickness. Don't go too thin. Periodically check to make sure the dough isn't sticking and sprinkle lightly with flour when it does. Using a 1½-inch (3.7-cm) cookie cutter, cut as many cookies out of the rolled dough as you can. Place the cookies on the parchment covered baking sheet, leaving 1 inch (2.5 cm) between cookies. Repeat with the other disc of dough, re-rolling the dough and cutting cookies until done. Use a chopstick or other small, round object to pierce a small hole out of the center of half of the cookies.

Place the cookies in the freezer for 15 to 20 minutes or the fridge for 30 to 40 minutes, and then take them directly from the freezer to the top rack of the oven and bake for 9 minutes. It's crucial not to overbake these. Let them cool for 5 minutes on the baking sheet and then transfer to a rack to finish cooling. Add 1 teaspoon of chilled jam to the center of each whole cookie and top with a cookie with the cut-out hole.

SPICED GINGERBREAD COOKIES TWO WAYS

My dad said "These are the best gingerbread cookies I've ever had." They are soft and chewy, not dry and crumbling. They roll out like a dream and taste of all kinds of spice. I included a glaze for when you want to make cute little gingerbread people and also a recipe for ginger buttercream for those days when you don't want to fuss with cutouts, but still crave gingerbread. Frankly, I was hesitant to put these in the holiday chapter because I feel like we need to break gingerbread free from its December chains and gorge on it year-round. Thoughts?

MAKES 42 (2-INCH [5-CM]) COOKIES

12 tablespoons (172 g) unsalted butter, room temperature

¾ cup (158 g) light or dark brown sugar, packed

¾ cup (180 ml) unsulphured molasses

1 large egg, room temperature

1 tablespoon (15 ml) milk

2 teaspoons (11 ml) real vanilla extract

2 cups (272 g) bread flour

1½ cups (204 g) all-purpose flour

1 tablespoon (8 g) ground ginger

3 teaspoons (8 g) cinnamon

½ teaspoon baking soda

1 teaspoon sea salt

1 teaspoon allspice

½ teaspoon cloves

½ teaspoon cardamom

½ teaspoon freshly grated nutmeg

To make the cookies, in an electric stand mixer fitted with the paddle attachment, add the butter and brown sugar and mix on medium for about 4 minutes, or until well blended. Add in the molasses, scraping down the sides and bottom of the bowl so that everything is incorporated. Continue to mix until smooth and add in the egg, milk and vanilla and mix for 2 minutes more.

In a medium bowl, whisk together the bread flour, all-purpose flour, ginger, cinnamon, baking soda, sea salt, allspice, cloves, cardamom and nutmeg. Add this to the molasses mixture and mix on low until blended. Separate into two equal halves and pat each mound of dough into a disc. Wrap tightly in plastic wrap and stash in the fridge for an hour or two, or up to several days, to rest.

Take the dough out of the fridge and let it sit for 10 minutes or longer to soften. Place it between two lightly floured layers of parchment. If you have a silicone baking mat, place it underneath the parchment to keep it from sliding on the counter. Roll the dough to ¼- to ½-inch (0.7- to 1.3-cm) thickness. If I'm using a round cutter, I go for thicker cookies. If I'm using detailed cookie cutters, I roll the dough a bit thinner.

Use the parchment to pull the dough onto a baking sheet and chill in the freezer for 15 minutes or the fridge for 30 minutes. This will make it easier to get clean cut outs.

Preheat the oven to 350°F (177°C) and cover several baking sheets with parchment paper.

Sprinkle a small bit of flour over the top of the dough and dip your cookie cutter in flour. Press as many shapes as possible on the dough. Place the cookies on the parchment covered baking sheet, leaving 1 inch (2.5 cm) between cookies, they won't spread much. Repeat with the other disc of dough, re-rolling the dough and cutting cookies until the dough is gone. I only like to gather scraps and re-roll once, so that the dough doesn't get tough.

Place the cookies in the freezer for 15 to 20 minutes or the fridge for 20 to 30 minutes and then take them directly from the freezer to the middle of the oven and bake for 8 to 9 minutes. It's crucial not to overbake these. Let them cool for 5 minutes on the baking sheet, and then transfer to a rack to finish cooling.

(continued)

GLAZE FOR HOLIDAY CUT-OUT COOKIES

2 cups (260 g) powdered sugar

4 tablespoons (60 ml) milk, or more to thin

1 teaspoon real vanilla extract

Gel food coloring, optional

Sprinkles, optional

GINGER BUTTERCREAM

8 tablespoons (115 g) butter, cut into 8 pieces, room temperature

2½ cups (325 g) powdered sugar

1 to 2 tablespoons (15 to 30 ml) milk

1½ tablespoons (23 g) candied ginger, finely chopped

To make the glaze, in a medium bowl, whisk the powdered sugar, milk, vanilla and any food coloring you're using until smooth. Either drizzle it over the cookies or dip the tops of each cookie in the glaze, letting the excess fall back into the bowl. Proceed with sprinkles or whatever your heart desires.

To make the buttercream, in an electric stand mixer fitted with the paddle, add the butter, powdered sugar, milk and ginger until smooth. Add more powdered sugar in 1-tablespoon (8-g) increments if the buttercream is too thin, or conversely, add more milk in 1 teaspoon increments if the buttercream is too thick. Smear over the tops of the cookies and enjoy!

PEPPERMINT CANDY MACARONS

I made batches upon batches of these macarons until I felt like I got the ingredients and technique just right for you. And I happened upon that magical combination on, of all days, Christmas. After we opened presents at my sister's I ran home to test this recipe more (because...deadlines) and I was doing backflips into Christmas dinner with a big pastry box overflowing with little peppermint macarons. The macaron shell is light and crispy and sandwiches the most delicious peppermint cream. My family loves these and I hope you will too! This is one recipe where I recommend you measure the ingredients by weight for more accuracy.

MAKES 50 MACARONS

1⅔ cups (210 g) powdered sugar

1½ cup plus scant 1 tablespoon (125 g) finely ground blanched almond meal

Roughly 4 large (130 g) egg whites

¼ teaspoon cream of tartar

½ cup (105 g) granulated sugar

¼ teaspoon peppermint extract

Food-safe gel coloring (I used Americolor Super Red 120)

Cover several baking sheets with parchment paper. Prepare your pastry bag by placing a round pastry tip in the bottom and place the bag in a large glass or vase to make it easier to fill. Prepare one more pastry bag with a round tip that you'll use later for the filling.

To make the cookies, add half of the powdered sugar to a food processor fitted with the blade attachment and top with the almond meal and the remainder of the powdered sugar. Pulse 6 to 8 times until no almond meal is visible. Set aside.

In an electric stand mixer fitted with the whisk attachment, add the egg whites and cream of tartar. Make sure the bowl and whisk are freshly cleaned and dried. Whisk on medium until the eggs are frothy and then slowly add in the granulated sugar. Turn the mixer on high and when the meringue is shiny and glossy and looks like marshmallow fluff, add in the peppermint extract. Turn the mixer back on high until you reach stiff peaks.

Sift the dry ingredients into the meringue in three batches, folding and mixing between each one. It should take around 20 folds for everything to get mixed together. Then spread the batter up the sides of the bowl and scoop it back down to the bottom. Repeat this about 3 times or until the mixture starts to slowly slump back down the sides of the bowl on its own.

Grab a clean paintbrush, dip it in the red food gel coloring and paint several stripes down the inside of your pasty bag. Keep them thin. Scoop the mixture into your prepared pastry bag and cut the bottom tip off.

Holding the pastry tip just above the baking sheet, press the batter into the shape of a dime, pause for a second and then quickly pull the pastry tip off to the side. You want the tops as smooth as possible. The macarons will spread a wee bit so leave about 1½ to 2 inches (3.7 to 5 cm) between each. Tap the pans 4 times on the counter to release any trapped bubbles and let sit for 20 to 45 minutes until they become dull and when gently touched no batter is transferred to your finger. This time will vary depending on local humidity. Use a toothpick to smooth out any air bubbles on the surface.

(continued)

PEPPERMINT FILLING

2 cups (260 g) powdered sugar

2 tablespoons (29 g) butter

1 tablespoon (14 g) vegetable shortening

2 to 3 tablespoons (29 to 44 ml) heavy whipping cream

3 tablespoons (30 g) finely crushed peppermint candy

½ teaspoon peppermint extract

Preheat the oven to 320°F (160°C) and bake the macarons for 11 minutes, or until they lift easily off of the parchment. Take care not to overbake them, they shouldn't darken or show any color change in the oven. Let cool completely.

To make the filling, in an electric stand mixer fitted with the paddle attachment, add the powdered sugar, butter, shortening and whipping cream and mix on low until combined, and then increase the speed to medium and mix until smooth. Add in the crushed candy and peppermint extract and mix for 1 minute more. Start with the minimum amount of cream and add more in 1-teaspoon increments to get to the desired consistency. You want the filling to be thick enough that it doesn't ooze out of the macaron, but moist enough that the cookies stick to it. Add this to your prepared pastry bag and pipe it into the center of half of the macarons. You want a nice, thick layer. Top with a macaron of equal size and you're done!

MACARON MAKING TIPS

- Watch your eggs when whisking them and don't over or under beat. You will have reached stiff peaks when you dip your whisk in the meringue and hold it upright. If the angle is at about 11:30, then it's just right. If it's at 12:00 they've been overbeaten. At 10:00, they need to be beaten more.

- Weigh your egg whites. I find the weight of large egg whites to be inconsistent, which can really throw the whole cookie off.

- Folding the dry ingredients into the meringue is a crucial step in successful macaron making. Drag your spatula down the middle of the batter and then run it along the side and flip the batter into the middle, turning the bowl a quarter turn with each fold. Do this about 20 times, or until the batter is mixed. Then spread the batter up the sides of the bowl to knock out any trapped bubbles and scoop it back into the bottom of the bowl. Do this about 3 times and the batter should start to slowly slump down the sides of the bowl. Now it's ready to pipe.

- When piping, hold your pastry bag perpendicular to the baking sheet and just slightly above it. The batter should be between the size of a dime and a nickel. Pause for a second and then quickly pull your pastry tip off to the side and away from the macaron.

- Make sure your baking sheets aren't warped and your parchment is lying flat.

- Watch your bake time! They should come off of the parchment easily when done, but they should have no color from the oven.

EGGNOG SNICKERDOODLES

I know, you don't have any rum extract in your cupboard. This is one of those occasions where I'm going to ask you to get out of your torn t-shirt and baggy sweats to run to the store and get some. It really does make this cookie. You should also grab some real eggnog and some proper rum to fix yourself a drink on the side.

MAKES 24 LARGE COOKIES

8 tablespoons (115 g) unsalted butter, room temperature

¾ cup (158 g) light brown sugar, packed

¾ cup (144 g) granulated sugar

2 large eggs, room temperature

¾ cup (177 ml) sunflower seed oil or other neutral oil

3 teaspoons (15 ml) real vanilla extract

1 teaspoon rum extract

1¾ cups (238 g) bread flour

1 cup (136 g) all-purpose flour

2 teaspoons (6 g) cream of tartar

1 teaspoon baking soda

1 teaspoon sea salt

1 teaspoon nutmeg

¾ teaspoon cinnamon

COOKIE COATING

¼ cup (48 g) granulated sugar

¾ teaspoon ground cinnamon

½ teaspoon nutmeg

To make the cookies, in an electric stand mixer fitted with the paddle attachment, add the butter, brown sugar and granulated sugar and mix on medium for 4 minutes or until light and fluffy. Add the eggs one at a time, scraping down the sides and bottom of the bowl and making sure they're fully blended before adding in the next. Add the oil, vanilla and rum extract and mix for 1 minute more.

In a medium-sized bowl, whisk together the bread flour, all-purpose flour, cream of tartar, baking soda, salt, nutmeg and cinnamon. Pour the flour mixture into the butter mixture, stirring to combine. Don't overmix, but make sure everything gets well blended together. I like to mix until the flour just disappears. Wrap tightly and shove in the fridge for several hours or until firm enough to roll.

Preheat your oven to 375°F (190°C) and place a rack in the top third of your oven, at least 6 inches (15 cm) from the heat source. Cover several baking sheets with parchment paper.

To make the cookie coating, in a small bowl, mix together the granulated sugar, cinnamon and nutmeg.

Take the dough out of the fridge and roll about 1½ tablespoons (21 g) of dough between your palms into a nice ball. Give the dough ball a generous coating of the sugar-spice mixture and set on the baking sheet. Make sure there are about 2 inches (5 cm) between each dough ball, allowing space for spreading during baking. Freeze the dough balls for 15 minutes, and then take from the freezer to the oven and bake for 11 minutes. Let them cool on the baking sheet for 10 minutes, and then finish cooling on a rack.

GET **STUFFED**

We could call this chapter Ode to a Sandwich Cookie. How do I love thee? Let me count the ways...I love thee smeared with frosting, loaded with ice cream, and coated with thick layers of jam...I'm not sure life gets much better.

I kick off this chapter with one of my all-time favorite confections: Mocha Sarah's (page 134). Sarah's were named for Sarah Bernhardt and are one of my most favorite childhood treats. They start with a light almond cookie topped with mocha French buttercream and then are dipped in chocolate until glossy. These are excellent when kept in the fridge and eaten on a warm day. Preferably alone, so you don't have to share.

The lemon-basil curd in the Lemon Basil Curd Butter Cookies (page 145) is absolutely, 100 percent not to be missed. The flavors are so bright and fresh. The perfect cookie to lift anyone's spirits.

Some tips to get you started:

- These are great recipes to make over several days if you're crunched for time. Make the ice cream one day and the cookies another. When it comes to ganache or buttercreams, I like to make those fresh, the day I plan to use them.

- Ice cream can merely be scooped and pressed between cookies or you can spread the ice cream on a rimmed baking sheet, keeping the surface even, and then freeze. Once frozen use cookie cutters, the size and shape of your cookies, to cut out chunks of ice cream. These look uber clean and chic and will have your friends wondering about your mad ice cream skills.

Shall we get stuffed?

MOCHA SARAH'S

Sarah's are Sarah Bernhardt Cookies...have you ever had one? They're composed of a simple almond cookie base, a French chocolate buttercream filling (I die) and a chocolate coating to seal the whole lot together. If you've never had one before the time has come. These are best stored in the fridge.

MAKES 30 COOKIES

5 ounces (142 g) almond paste

⅓ cup (64 g) granulated sugar

1 large egg white, room temperature

½ teaspoon almond extract

¼ teaspoon sea salt

MOCHA FILLING

½ cup (96 g) granulated sugar

⅓ cup (75 ml) water, room temperature

4 large egg yolks

¼ cup (21 g) unsweetened dark (Dutch process) cocoa powder, sifted

24 tablespoons (344 g) unsalted butter, cut into 24 chunks, room temperature

1 teaspoon finely ground espresso or coffee (not instant coffee)

CHOCOLATE GLAZE

3 cups (360 g) dark chocolate, finely chopped

2 tablespoons (28 g) vegetable shortening

To make the cookies, preheat your oven to 350°F (177°C) and cover a baking sheet with parchment paper. Place the almond paste and sugar in an electric stand mixer fitted with the paddle attachment, and mix on medium for 4 to 5 minutes. It will be integrated, but not smooth. Add in the egg white, almond extract and salt and run the mixer on medium high for several minutes until the mixture comes together. This mixture will be unlike typical cookie dough but don't worry. Either use a pastry bag fitted with a round tip, or use two spoons to make 1-inch (2.5-cm) diameter mounds, leaving 1½ inches (3.7 cm) between them. Bake one sheet at a time in the center of the oven for 10 minutes. Let them cool on the baking sheet for 10 minutes and then transfer to a rack to finish cooling. Once cool, return to the parchment-covered baking sheet and invert the cookies so that the flat bottoms are facing up.

To make the filling, add the sugar and water to a medium saucepan over medium-low heat and cook for 20 minutes or until it reaches 240°F (115°C). The sugar will be completely dissolved, but it should not have changed color. Keep an eye on it so that it doesn't start to darken. Don't stir as you don't want to splash the liquid up the sides of the pan.

When the sugar water is almost ready, add the egg yolks to an electric stand mixer fitted with the whisk attachment and whisk on high for 4 minutes, or until they have lightened in color. When the sugar is ready, turn the mixer on medium low and slowly stream the screaming-hot sugar water in towards the side of the bowl; be careful not to hit the whisk. Add in the cocoa powder with the mixer on low until incorporated, and then turn the mixer on high until the bottom of the bowl feels cool. Once cool, turn the mixer down to medium and add in the butter, one chunk at a time, making sure it is completely blended before adding in the next chunk. Add in the ground espresso and run the machine for 1 minute more. Using a pastry bag fitted with a round tip, or using two spoons, make a mound of the filling on top of each almond cookie and place the baking sheet in the freezer for 1 hour. If the sheet won't fit in your freezer, place the cookies on plates.

To make the chocolate glaze, in a medium, heat-safe bowl add the chocolate and shortening and set over a medium saucepan of simmering water. Do not let the bowl touch the water or let the water boil. Stir frequently until melted and smooth. Place a towel on the counter, take the bowl off of the heat and set the bowl on top of the towel. Stir every couple of minutes. Once cool, invert the frozen cookies and dip just the filling (and not the cookie) into the chocolate, letting the excess fall back into the bowl. Set them back on the baking sheet for the chocolate to set.

THE HOLY SH!T S'MORE COOKIE

This recipe got its name because "Holy Sh!t" is what I said when I took my first bite of this cookie. It's that yummy. This recipe is a blog favorite and it's the perfect summer treat for when you can't be bothered with a campfire. I personally like to really char my marshmallows because it brings out that campfire flavor, and also the meltier the marshmallows are when they are smooshed between the cookies, the more readily they'll spread and let the graham crumbs stick to the sides.

MAKES 18 SANDWICHES

1¾ cups (210 g) semisweet chocolate, coarsely chopped

½ cup (118 ml) sunflower seed oil or other neutral oil

3 large eggs, room temperature

2 teaspoons (11 ml) pure vanilla extract

¾ cup (158 g) light brown sugar, packed

¾ cup (144 g) granulated sugar

1 cup (136 g) bread flour

¾ cup (103 g) all-purpose flour

¼ cup (21 g) unsweetened dark (Dutch process) cocoa powder

1½ teaspoons (6 g) baking powder

1 teaspoon baking soda

1½ teaspoons (7 g) sea salt

1½ cups (180 g) dark chocolate chips

36 regular-sized marshmallows

½ cup (60 g) graham crackers (about 4 whole graham crackers), finely ground

Melt the chocolate and oil in the microwave in a large microwave-safe bowl or in a double boiler. I usually do 1 minute on high, but microwaves are funky so keep an eye on things. Stir the chocolate to get rid of any chunks. Sometimes it will look chunky, but if you give it 20 or so stirs with a wooden spoon, you'll get rid of all of the chunks without burning it. Whisk in the eggs, one at a time, making sure each is completely blended before adding in the next. Whisk in the vanilla extract, brown sugar and granulated sugar. Set aside.

In a medium bowl, whisk together the bread flour, all-purpose flour, cocoa powder, baking powder, baking soda and salt. Pour into the chocolate mixture, stirring until just combined. Fold in the chocolate chips until equally distributed throughout. Wrap tightly and chill for 30 minutes in the fridge.

Preheat your oven to 350°F (177°C) and line your cookie sheets with parchment paper. Roll together 2 tablespoons (28 g) of dough and allow at least 2 inches (5 cm) between the dough balls. Try to make them as spherical as possible and equal in size so they will pair up nicely when smooshing the marshmallows. Freeze the dough balls for 10 minutes or place in the fridge for 20 minutes.

Bake one sheet at a time in the center of the oven for 11 minutes. You want to slightly underbake these. Allow the cookies to cool on the sheet for 5 to 10 minutes, or until they come off easily.

Turn on your oven broiler. Make sure you have everything ready for when the marshmallows come out, because you will need to act quickly. This means you should have the graham crackers chopped and your cookies open-face and ready to be paired up.

Put the marshmallows on a parchment-lined baking sheet and char under the broiler for 1 minute, then flip them and broil for 1 minute more. Keep an eye on them, they will burn on a dime. Place 2 charred marshmallows between 2 cookies, press down and then roll the sides in your graham cracker crumbs. Let me just tell you: this is an imperfect process. Not all of the sides of the marshmallow will be wet enough to hold the crumbs, so there will be some bald spots. I'm ok with that. One other tip: when you are sandwiching the marshmallows between the cookies, twist the cookies as you press down. This will force the marshmallow to fill the inside of the cookie instead of overflowing out.

THE DEFIBRILLATOR

My love of espresso is only matched by my unabashed love for and addiction to chocolate. The two together are simply perfection. A thin, but chewy and soft cookie smashes what can only be described as the PERFECT espresso cream. I can't stress enough how much you're going to love this cookie. If you love espresso or strong coffee, you'll love this one. If not, keep moving along. This one's not for you.

MAKES 10 (3½-INCH [8.7-CM]) COOKIE SANDWICHES

1¼ cups (150 g) semisweet chocolate, coarsely chopped

½ cup (118 ml) sunflower seed oil or other neutral oil

3 large eggs, room temperature

1 cup (210 g) light brown sugar, packed

½ cup (96 g) granulated sugar

1 tablespoon (15 ml) freshly brewed espresso

1¼ cups (170 g) bread flour

½ cup (68 g) all-purpose flour

¼ cup (21 g) unsweetened dark (Dutch process) cocoa powder

1½ teaspoons (7 g) sea salt

1 teaspoon baking powder

¾ teaspoon baking soda

ESPRESSO CREAM

8 tablespoons (115 g) unsalted butter, room temperature

¼ cup (55 g) vegetable shortening

3½ cups (455 g) powdered sugar

1 tablespoon (6 g) ground espresso

2 teaspoons (8 ml) freshly brewed espresso

1 tablespoon (15 ml) milk, or more to thin

To make the cookies, place the chocolate and oil in a medium microwave-safe bowl and microwave on high in 30 second increments, stirring in between, until the chocolate is melted, but still has some visible chunks. Stir until smooth. Let cool slightly and then whisk in your eggs, brown sugar, granulated sugar and espresso.

In another medium bowl, whisk together the bread flour, all-purpose flour, cocoa powder, sea salt, baking powder and baking soda. Pour the flour mixture into the chocolate mixture and give a couple of stirs until the dough is just starting to come together. Wrap tightly and chill the cookie dough for 20 to 30 minutes in the fridge.

Preheat your oven to 375°F (190°C) and place a rack in the top third of your oven, no less than 6 inches (15 cm) from the heat source. Line your baking sheets with parchment paper.

Gently roll 2 tablespoons (28 g) of dough into a ball and place it on the cookie sheet, allowing about 2 inches (5 cm) between each dough ball. Bake one sheet at a time in the top third of the oven for 9 minutes. You want to slightly underbake these. Allow the cookies to cool on the sheet for 15 minutes then transfer to a cooling rack.

To make the espresso cream, while the cookies are cooling, place the butter and shortening in an electric stand mixer fitted with the paddle attachment. Mix on medium until well blended. Add in the powdered sugar, ground espresso, freshly brewed espresso and milk and mix on low until nice and creamy.

Pair up cookies that are of equal sizes. Give a generous (I mean it) smear of espresso cream on one side and smash another cookie on top. If you want it to look nice and tidy, run a finger around the outside of the cream to smooth it out.

TIPS

- You can substitute fresh-brewed strong coffee for the espresso.
- For the Espresso Cream, use actual ground espresso, not instant espresso. I use a Nespresso pod and it works great.

PETITE CARAMEL CREAMS

You're seriously going to wonder where caramel cream has been your whole life. It's like caramel, but thicker and more like frosting. These cookies are sweet, petite and sparkle like a prize. The ample amount this recipe produces make these the perfect cookie for a dessert table or to take to a party.

MAKES 52 SANDWICHES

CARAMEL CREAM

8 tablespoons (115 g) unsalted butter

1 cup (210 g) light brown sugar, packed

¼ teaspoon sea salt

⅓ cup (79 ml) whole milk, or more to thin

1 teaspoon vanilla bean paste or real vanilla extract

2 cups (260 g) powdered sugar

SANDWICH COOKIE

8 tablespoons (115 g) unsalted butter, room temperature

1¼ cups (263 g) light brown sugar, packed

½ cup (96 g) granulated sugar

2 large eggs, room temperature

1 large egg yolk, room temperature

3 teaspoons (15 ml) real vanilla extract

½ cup (118 ml) sunflower seed oil or other neutral oil

1¼ cups (170 g) bread flour

1 cup (136 g) all-purpose flour

⅔ cup (56 g) unsweetened dark (Dutch process) cocoa powder

1 teaspoon baking powder

1 teaspoon sea salt

COOKIE COATING

½ cup (96 g) sparkling sugar

To make the cream, place the butter, brown sugar and salt in a medium heavy-bottomed saucepan over medium heat, stirring until melted. Crank up the heat to medium high, continue stirring and bring the mixture to a boil. Take off of the heat and slowly whisk in the milk and vanilla. Return to the heat, continue stirring and bring to a boil once more. Remove from the heat and let cool for 25 minutes. Stir in the powdered sugar. Sometimes I throw it in the electric stand mixer fitted with the paddle attachment to blend smoothly. Add more milk, in 1 teaspoon increments, if the cream is too thick. Set aside.

To make the cookies, in an electric stand mixer fitted with the paddle attachment, add the butter, brown sugar and granulated sugar and mix on medium for 4 minutes or until light and well blended. Add in the eggs and egg yolk, one at a time, taking care that each is well blended before adding in the next. Add in the vanilla and oil, running the machine 1 minute more or until thoroughly blended. Take the bowl out of the mixer.

In a medium bowl, whisk together the bread flour, all-purpose flour, cocoa powder, baking powder and sea salt. Add this to the butter mixture and combine in as few strokes as possible and until no flour streaks remain. Wrap tightly and chill for at least 3 hours or until it's firmed up a bit.

Preheat the oven to 350°F (177°C) and cover several baking sheets with parchment paper.

For the cookie coating, place the sparkling sugar in a small, shallow bowl.

Roll 2 teaspoons (10 g) of dough into little balls and then roll in the sparkling sugar to cover completely. Set on the prepared baking sheet leaving a 1½-inch (3.7-cm) space between dough balls. Place in the freezer for 10 minutes prior to baking. If the dough gets sticky while rolling, place it in the freezer for 10 minutes to firm back up.

Bake one sheet at a time for 8 minutes in the center of the oven. Let cool for 5 minutes on the baking sheet, and then transfer to a rack to finish cooling.

To assemble, pair similar-sized cookies, smearing some caramel cream on one half and pressing the other cookie on top. Repeat with the remaining cookies. You will have leftover caramel cream. Store it in the fridge and reserve for another use.

ORANGE SCENTED BUTTER COOKIES
WITH CHOCOLATE GANACHE

This cookie has morphed over time from a piped cookie to a slice-and-bake cookie to the rolled-out cookie it is today: a petite, fluted rectangle cookie. I have to say, hands-down this is the easiest and prettiest iteration of all of the different methods. She's sandy and buttery, loaded with lots of orange zest and finished with a layer of thick ganache. Ain't NOTHING wrong with that.

MAKES 20 PETITE SANDWICH COOKIES

16 tablespoons (230 g) unsalted butter, cut into 16 pieces, room temperature

¾ cup (98 g) powdered sugar

1½ tablespoons (14 g) orange zest

1 large egg, room temperature

1 large egg yolk, room temperature

1½ teaspoons (7 ml) real vanilla extract

½ teaspoon sea salt

2 cups (272 g) all-purpose flour

GANACHE

1 cup (120 g) dark chocolate, finely chopped

¾ cup (177 ml) heavy whipping cream

If your butter isn't super soft, soften it in the microwave on high for 5 to 10 seconds. Cover several baking sheets with parchment paper.

In an electric stand mixer fitted with the paddle, add the butter, powdered sugar and orange zest and run the machine on medium for 4 minutes or until smooth. With the machine on low, add in the egg, egg yolk, vanilla and salt and run the machine for several minutes more. The mixture may look curdled. Dump in the flour and run the machine on the lowest setting until the dough comes together.

Lay a silicone baking mat on the counter and then place a piece of parchment paper on top, lightly flouring it. Set the dough on top and sprinkle with a bit more flour. Rub some flour over your rolling pin and roll the dough to ¼-inch (0.7-cm) thickness. Use the parchment paper to transfer it to a baking sheet and let chill in the freezer for 30 minutes or in the refrigerator for 1 hour.

Use a 1¼ x 1½–inch (3.3 x 3.7–cm) fluted rectangle cookie cutter and cut as many rectangles as possible. Gather the scraps and re-roll and cut as many cookies as you can. Chill in the freezer for 15 minutes or the fridge for 30 minutes.

Preheat your oven to 350°F (177°C).

Bake one sheet at a time in the center of the oven for 8 minutes. Let cool on the baking sheet for 5 minutes and then transfer to a rack to finish cooling.

To make the ganache, in a medium, heat-safe bowl add the chocolate and cream and set over a medium saucepan of simmering water. Do not let the bowl touch the water or let the water boil. Stir frequently until melted and smooth. Take off of the heat and stir every couple of minutes to help it cool, stay fluid and thicken. Once the cookies and the chocolate have both cooled smear an ample amount of chocolate on one cookie and top with another. Done!

LEMON BASIL CURD BUTTER COOKIES

Sweet baby Jesus where have these been all my life? These are bright and lemony with the infusion of fresh basil transforming them to sublime. Maybe even otherworldly. I chose a large cut-out for the top cookie to highlight the vibrancy of the curd. These will quickly become a favorite. Promise.

MAKES 32 SANDWICH COOKIES

LEMON BASIL CURD

1 cup (192 g) granulated sugar

2 tablespoons (19 g) lemon zest

4 tablespoons (33 g) powdered sugar

2 large eggs

1 large egg yolk

⅓ cup (79 ml) fresh lemon juice (about 2 to 3 lemons)

⅓ cup (45 g) all-purpose flour

¼ cup (6 g) fresh basil, tightly packed

2 tablespoons (29 g) unsalted butter, room temperature

BUTTER COOKIE

16 tablespoons (230 g) unsalted butter, room temperature

¾ cup (98 g) powdered sugar

1½ tablespoons (14 g) lemon zest

1 large egg, room temperature

1 large egg yolk, room temperature

1 tablespoon (15 ml) milk, room temperature

1½ teaspoons (7 ml) real vanilla extract

½ teaspoon sea salt

2 cups (272 g) all-purpose flour

To make the curd, place the granulated sugar and lemon zest in the bowl of a food processor fitted with the blade and pulse several times to combine. Add in the powdered sugar, eggs, egg yolk and lemon juice and run the machine for 30 to 60 seconds or until combined. Add in the flour and run the machine for 30 seconds more.

Strain the mixture into a heavy-bottomed saucepan over medium heat. Add the basil and butter and stir constantly for 6 to 8 minutes or until thickened. Strain once again if the mixture developed any lumps and immediately place in a small, heat-safe bowl and cover with plastic wrap, directly on the surface of the curd. Place in the fridge to chill completely.

To make the cookies, if your butter isn't super soft, heat it in the microwave on high for 5 to 10 seconds. In an electric stand mixer fitted with the paddle, add the butter, powdered sugar and lemon zest and run the machine on medium for 4 minutes or until smooth. With the machine on low, add in the egg, egg yolk, milk, vanilla and salt and run the machine on low for several minutes more. Make sure to scrape down the sides and bottom of the bowl so that everything is incorporated. The mixture may look curdled. Dump in the flour and run the machine on the lowest setting until the dough comes together.

Place a silicone baking mat on the counter and then place a piece of parchment paper on top, lightly flouring it. Set the dough on top and sprinkle with a bit more flour. Rub some flour over your rolling pin and roll the dough to ¼-inch (0.7-cm) thickness. Use the parchment paper to transfer it onto a baking sheet and chill in the freezer for 15 to 20 minutes or in the refrigerator for 30 to 40 minutes.

Preheat your oven to 350°F (177°C) and line several baking sheets with parchment paper. Grab a 1¾-inch (4.5-cm) round cookie cutter and a 1¼-inch (3.3-cm) round cookie cutter. Cut as many 1¾-inch (4.5-cm) circles out of the dough as you can. Re-roll the scraps and cut as many from that dough. Use the 1¼-inch (3.3-cm) cutter to cut smaller circles out of half of the 1¾-inch (4.5-cm) circles. Place all of the cookies, including the small circles from the cut-out cookies, on the prepared baking sheets with 1½ inches (3.7 cm) between each cookie, and freeze for 10 minutes or refrigerate for 20 minutes.

Bake one sheet at a time in the center of the oven for 8 to 9 minutes. Let cool on the baking sheet. To assemble, for the larger cookies, smear some curd on the solid circle and top with an 'O' shaped cookie. For the smaller cookies, smear some curd on one cookie and top with a same-sized cookie.

SMOKED CHOCOLATE COOKIES

I literally died (actually I didn't) when I tasted these. These are delicious as-is, or you can dip the cookies in melted bittersweet chocolate and sprinkle with more smoked salt if you're feeling really frisky, like I did for the photos.

16 SANDWICHES

ICE CREAM

1 cup (170 g) raw hazelnuts, toasted and coarsely chopped

1⅓ cups (256 g) granulated sugar

1½ cups (355 ml) whole milk

3 tablespoons (28 g) cornstarch

2 tablespoons (14 g) unsweetened dark (Dutch process) cocoa powder

⅔ cup (80 g) dark chocolate, finely chopped

2 large eggs

1½ cups (355 ml) heavy cream

1 teaspoon vanilla bean paste or real vanilla extract

1 teaspoon sea salt

SANDWICH COOKIE

24 tablespoons (344 g) unsalted butter, room temperature

1 cup (192 g) granulated sugar

½ cup (105 g) light brown sugar, packed

2 large eggs, room temperature

2 teaspoons (11 ml) pure vanilla extract

3 cups (408 g) bread flour

½ cup (68 g) all-purpose flour

½ cup (43 g) unsweetened dark (Dutch process) cocoa powder

1 teaspoon baking powder

1 teaspoon baking soda

2 teaspoons (10 g) fine smoked sea salt

2 to 3 tablespoons (10 to 15 g) smoked sea salt flakes

To make the ice cream, add the hazelnuts and sugar to a food processor fitted with the blade attachment and run the machine for about 6 to 8 minutes or until fully incorporated and no hazelnut chunks remain. Transfer the mixture to a large, heavy-bottomed saucepan over medium heat and whisk in the milk, cornstarch and cocoa powder. At this point, you can strain the mixture and return it to the saucepan if the consistency isn't smooth enough. Turn the heat up to high and bring the mixture to a boil, whisking until thickened. Take it off of the heat and add the chocolate, stirring to melt. Add in the eggs, one at a time, constantly whisking to keep them from scrambling. Finally, whisk in the heavy cream, vanilla and salt. Transfer to a lidded container and put in the fridge until chilled through, about 2 to 3 hours.

Add the mixture to an ice cream maker and follow the manufacturer's instructions. Store in a lidded container in the freezer until ready to use.

To make the cookies, in an electric stand mixer fitted with the paddle attachment, mix the butter, granulated sugar and brown sugar on medium for 4 minutes or until light and fluffy. With the mixer on low add in the eggs, one at a time, scraping down the sides and bottom of the bowl and making sure each is fully blended before adding the next. Add in the vanilla and mix for 1 minute more, or until fully blended.

In a large bowl, whisk together the bread flour, all-purpose flour, cocoa powder, baking powder, baking soda and fine smoked sea salt. Add to the butter mixture and stir until just blended. Separate into two equal halves and pat each mound of dough into a disc.

Place the dough between two layers of parchment. Lightly cover the top and bottom of the dough with a dusting of unsweetened cocoa powder. If you have a silicone baking mat, place it underneath the parchment to keep it from sliding on the counter. Roll the dough to ½-inch (1.3-cm) thickness. Don't go too thin. Periodically check to make sure the dough isn't sticking and sprinkle lightly with more cocoa powder when it does. Repeat with the second disc of dough.

(continued)

GARNISH

¾ cup (90 g) dark chocolate

1 tablespoon (14 g) vegetable shortening

With the dough on the parchment, transfer it to a baking sheet and place in the freezer for 30 minutes or the fridge for 1 hour to firm up. You can stack the dough with the parchment between layers.

Preheat the oven to 350°F (177°C) and cover several baking sheets with parchment paper. If your only baking sheet is the one in the freezer, that's fine, you can use it when the dough is properly chilled. Place a rack in the top third of the oven at least 6 inches from the heat source.

Once chilled, using a 2 x 2¾-inch (5 x 7-cm) fluted rectangle cookie cutter, cut as many cookies out of the rolled dough as you can. Place the cookies on the parchment covered baking sheet, leaving 1 inch (2.5 cm) between cookies. Repeat with the other disc of dough, re-rolling dough and cutting cookies until done. Place the cookies in the freezer for 15 to 20 minutes or the fridge for 30 to 40 minutes, and then take them directly to the top rack of the oven and bake for 9 minutes. It's crucial not to overbake these. Let them cool for 5 minutes on the baking sheet and then transfer to a rack to finish cooling.

For the garnish, while the cookies cool, in a medium, heat-safe bowl add the chocolate and shortening and set over a medium saucepan of simmering water. Do not let the bowl touch the water or let the water come to a boil. Stir frequently until melted and smooth. Place a towel on the counter and set the bowl on top of it. Dip the top half of the cooled cookies into the chocolate, letting the excess fall back into the bowl. Repeat with half of the cookies as only the top half of the ice cream sandwiches will be dipped in chocolate. Sprinkle with smoked sea salt flakes and let the chocolate set.

To assemble, let the ice cream soften on the counter for 5 minutes, if necessary. Scoop a ½ cup (113 g) of ice cream onto the bottom of one cookie and top with a chocolate dipped cookie. Gently press down until the ice cream comes to the edges of the cookies. If you want to be really specific about it, you can line a small rimmed baking sheet with parchment paper and evenly spread the ice cream, about 1-inch (2.5-cm) thick, over the top. Freeze until firm and then use the same cookie cutter you used for the cookies to cut out the ice cream. Store the sandwiches in the freezer, wrapped tightly in an airtight container, until ready to serve. This recipe makes an ample amount of ice cream so you'll have leftovers to enjoy.

BLACK FOREST ICE CREAM SAMMIES

Two chocolate-cherry cookies smoosh together with a center of heavenly ice cream comprised of even more cherries and chocolate. There is no part of this cookie that doesn't make me extremely happy. I recommend making the ice cream in advance so it has time to chill and firm up a bit. I tend to formulate my ice cream so that it never gets rock hard and always maintains a fair degree of softness. This makes it especially receptive to sandwich smooshing.

MAKES 14 TO 16 (2½-INCH [6.3-CM]) SANDWICHES

ICE CREAM

1 cup (120 g) dark chocolate, finely chopped

1 tablespoon (14 g) vegetable shortening

1 cup (237 ml) whole milk

¾ cup (144 g) granulated sugar

1 vanilla bean, split and scraped

1 cup (237 ml) heavy cream

2 large eggs

1 teaspoon sea salt

1½ cups (149 g) drained dark cherries in light syrup, reserve 1 tablespoon (15 ml) for the cookies, cherries coarsely chopped*

*Use paper towels to blot excess moisture from the cherries.

To make the ice cream, cover a rimmed baking sheet with parchment paper.

In a medium, heat-safe bowl add the chocolate and shortening and set over a medium saucepan of simmering water. Do not let the bowl touch the water or let the water come to a boil. Stir frequently until melted and smooth. Spread the melted chocolate over the parchment paper in a thin layer about ¼-inch (0.7-cm) thick. Place in the freezer. Once chilled, chop into small bits and place back in the freezer until ready to add to the ice cream.

Place the milk and sugar in a large, heavy-bottomed saucepan over medium heat and whisk until the sugar is melted. Take it off of the heat and add in the scraped vanilla bean seeds and the cream. Add in the eggs, one at a time, constantly whisking. Stir in the salt and transfer to a lidded container and put in the fridge until chilled through, about 2 to 3 hours.

Add the mixture to an ice cream maker and follow the manufacturer's instructions, adding in the chopped chocolate and cherries once the mixture is thick and the ice cream is just about done. Run the machine for several minutes more, or until the cherries and chocolate are evenly distributed throughout. Store in a lidded container in the freezer until ready to use.

(continued)

SANDWICH COOKIE

1¾ cups (210 g) semisweet chocolate, coarsely chopped

½ cup (118 ml) sunflower oil or other neutral oil

1 cup (210 g) brown sugar, packed

½ cup (96 g) granulated sugar

1 tablespoon (15 ml) reserved cherry syrup

1 teaspoon real vanilla extract

3 large eggs, room temperature

1 cup (136 g) bread flour

¾ cup (103 g) all-purpose flour

¼ cup (21 g) unsweetened cocoa powder

1 teaspoon baking powder

1 teaspoon baking soda

1½ teaspoons (7 g) sea salt

2 cups (331 g) dried tart cherries

To make the cookies, in a medium, heat-safe bowl add the chocolate and oil and set over a medium saucepan of simmering water. Do not let the bowl touch the water or let the water come to a boil. Stir frequently until melted and smooth. Take off of the heat and whisk in the brown sugar, granulated sugar, cherry syrup, vanilla and add the eggs, one at a time, making sure each is well blended before adding in the next.

In a medium bowl, whisk together the bread flour, all-purpose flour, cocoa powder, baking powder, baking soda and sea salt. Pour the flour mixture into the chocolate mixture and stir until just combined. Fold in the cherries until they are evenly distributed.

Preheat your oven to 375°F (190°C). Line your baking sheets with parchment paper.

Roll 1½ tablespoons (21 g) of dough and place on the baking sheet, allowing 2 inches (5 cm) between dough balls. Freeze for 10 minutes or place in the fridge for 20 minutes.

Bake one sheet at a time for 10 minutes in the center of the oven. You want to slightly underbake these. Allow the cookies to cool on the sheet for 5 to 10 minutes, or until they come off easily, and transfer to a rack to finish cooling.

To assemble, let the ice cream soften on the counter for 5 minutes. Scoop ⅓ cup (76 g) of ice cream onto the bottom of one cookie and top with another right-side up cookie. Gently press down until the ice cream comes to the edges of the cookies. If you want to be really specific about it, you can line a small rimmed baking sheet with parchment paper and evenly spread the ice cream, about 1-inch (2.5-cm) thick, over the top. Freeze until firm and then use a cookie cutter or edge of glass that is a bit smaller than the circumference of the cookie to cut out ice cream rounds. Remove from the baking sheet and place on the cookies as noted above.

Store the sandwiches in the freezer, wrapped tightly in an airtight container, until ready to serve.

MANDARIN ORANGE CREAM SAMMIES

Stella absolutely loves these! If you have a soft spot for orange cream popsicles, this sammy is for you. The cookies are big and puffy and citrusy and the overarching flavor profile is orange and vanilla. Ain't nothing wrong with that.

MAKES 8 JUMBO SAMMIES

ICE CREAM

1 cup (237 ml) whole milk

¾ cup (144 g) granulated sugar

2 tablespoons (30 ml) fresh orange juice

2 tablespoons (19 g) orange zest

¾ teaspoons orange blossom water

1½ teaspoons (7 ml) real vanilla extract

½ teaspoon sea salt

1 cup (237 ml) heavy whipping cream

2 large eggs, room temperature

SANDWICH COOKIE

8 tablespoons (115 g) unsalted butter, room temperature

¾ cup (158 g) light brown sugar, packed

¾ cup (144 g) granulated sugar

2 large eggs, room temperature

3 tablespoons (28 g) orange zest

1 teaspoon (5 ml) orange blossom water

1½ teaspoons (7 ml) real vanilla extract

¾ cup (177 ml) sunflower seed oil or other neutral oil

1¾ cups (238 g) bread flour

1 cup (136 g) all-purpose flour

1 teaspoon baking powder

1 teaspoon baking soda

1 teaspoon sea salt

COOKIE COATING

½ cup (96 g) granulated sugar

To make the ice cream, place the milk and sugar in a medium saucepan over medium heat and whisk until the sugar is melted. Take it off of the heat and stir in the orange juice, orange zest, orange blossom water, vanilla, salt and whipping cream. Whisk in the eggs, one at a time, making sure each is well blended before adding in the next. Transfer the mixture to a lidded container and put in the fridge until chilled through, about 2 to 3 hours.

Add the mixture to an ice cream maker and follow the manufacturer's instructions. Store in a lidded container in the freezer until ready to use.

To make the cookies, preheat your oven to 350°F (177°C) and cover several baking sheets in parchment paper. In an electric stand mixer fitted with the paddle attachment, add the butter, brown sugar and granulated sugar and mix on medium for about 4 minutes, or until light and fluffy. Add in the eggs, one at a time, taking care to make sure each is well blended before adding the next. Add in the orange zest, orange blossom water and vanilla and mix for 1 minute more. Finally, with the mixer on low, stream in the oil and continue running the machine until it is completely combined. Take the bowl out of the mixer and set aside.

In a medium bowl, whisk together the bread flour, all-purpose flour, baking powder, baking soda and salt. Add to the butter mixture, stirring until just combined. For the cookie coating, in a shallow bowl add the sugar and set aside. Roll 2½ tablespoons (30 g) of dough into a ball and then roll in the sugar to coat completely. Set on the prepared baking sheet leaving 1½ inches (3.7 cm) between dough balls. Bake one sheet at a time in the center of the oven for 11 to 12 minutes. Let cool completely on the baking sheet.

To assemble, let the ice cream soften on the counter for 5 minutes. Scoop ½ cup (113 g) of ice cream onto the bottom of one cookie and top with another right-side up cookie. Gently press down until the ice cream comes to the edges of the cookies. If you want to be really specific about it, you can line a small rimmed baking sheet with parchment paper and evenly spread the ice cream, about 1-inch (2.5-cm) thick, over the top. Freeze until firm and then use a cookie cutter or edge of glass that is a bit smaller than the circumference of the cookie to cut out ice cream rounds. Remove from the baking sheet and place on the cookies as noted above. Store the sandwiches in the freezer, wrapped tightly in an airtight container, until ready to serve.

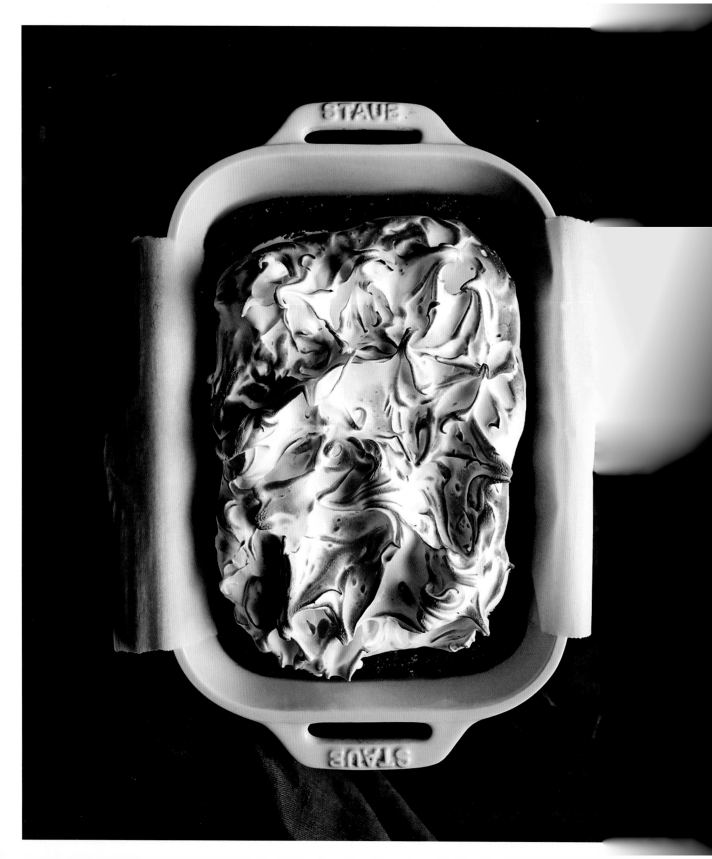

HEAVENLY
BAR COOKIES

Bar cookies are that delicious trifecta of cookie baking: they require only one bake time (no waiting for trays to cool before you put more dough on them), they dirty one casserole dish (read: fewer dishes to wash later) and they often appear to be a cake masquerading as a cookie, but we don't care. As long as we can torch meringue and slather on some buttercream, there's no need to split hairs.

I sincerely love a good blondie or brownie. They're the original bar cookies. But they're really just the beginning. I took the inspiration for Chocolate Espresso Cream Bars (page 164) from a dinner I had at the Farmstead in St. Helena with a bunch of fellow bloggers (make sure you try their Chocolate Cream Pie). A trip to Thailand inspired Stella's Thai Lemongrass Lime Bars (page 160). Heaps of inspiration comes from cakes...Carrot Cake Bars (page 172) anyone?

Before I send you off and running to make bar cookies, I want to arm you with these bar cookie universal truths:

1. Bar cookies always (ALWAYS) cut nicer and taste better when cooled completely.

2. If the dough is particularly thick, press it down gently and evenly with damp (not wet) hands.

3. If you go up or down in the pan size, rather than using the recommended pan size, you need to adjust bake time accordingly. Additionally, these were tested in ceramic pans. If you use a metal pan check earlier for doneness as it could affect the baking time.

4. Grease your pans how you please and then line with parchment paper. Let's talk parchment paper, shall we? You want a nice, long piece that lays flat on the bottom of the pan, is trimmed so it doesn't get bunched up in the corners and has at least a 1-inch (2.5-cm) overhang on each opposing side to be used as handles to pull your cooled bars out of the pan. To help get the parchment to lay flat, spray underneath and over the top with nonstick spray and press to the pan.

I've never met anyone that doesn't like bar cookies. If you find someone that doesn't, continue along on your life path without them.

LEMON RASPBERRY SUMMER BARS

These were completely inspired by my favorite raspberry scones. I wanted to see streaks of fresh raspberries laced throughout the bar with a fresh pop of lemon in every bite. These are soft, flirting with the idea of being an afternoon cake, but pausing just at the line. They're begging for a spot of tea, perhaps with a hit of bourbon. If you happen to have a wraparound porch I'll be right over.

MAKES ABOUT 18 BARS

1½ cups (288 g) granulated sugar

8 tablespoons (115 g) unsalted butter, melted

2 large eggs, room temperature

1 egg yolk, room temperature

⅓ cup (79 ml) sunflower seed oil or other neutral oil

4 tablespoons (36 g) lemon zest

2 tablespoons (30 ml) milk, room temperature

2 teaspoons (11 ml) real vanilla extract

1½ cups (204 g) bread flour

1½ cups (204 g) all-purpose flour

2 teaspoons (7 g) baking powder

1 teaspoon baking soda

1 teaspoon cinnamon

1 teaspoon sea salt

12 ounces (336 g) fresh raspberries

LEMON GLAZE

1½ cups (195 g) powdered sugar

1 tablespoon (9 g) lemon zest

1 tablespoon (15 ml) fresh lemon juice

1 to 3 tablespoons (15 to 45 ml) milk, or more to thin

Preheat your oven to 375°F (190°C). Grease a 9 x 13–inch (23 x 33–cm) casserole dish and line with parchment paper, letting the excess fall over the sides.

Whisk together the granulated sugar, butter, eggs, egg yolk, oil, lemon zest, milk and vanilla until thoroughly blended.

In another medium bowl, whisk together the bread flour, all-purpose flour, baking powder, baking soda, cinnamon and sea salt. Add to the butter mixture and stir until barely blended. Add in the raspberries and continue to blend until just combined and the raspberries are evenly distributed. It's okay if they bleed a bit. The dough will be thick.

Spoon the dough into the prepared baking dish. Dampen your hands and gently press down so that it covers the bottom of the dish. Bake in the center of the oven for 35 to 40 minutes. It will continue to cook and firm up as it cools. Let it cool completely.

To make the glaze, in a small bowl, whisk together the powdered sugar, lemon zest and lemon juice, and add in the milk, 1 tablespoon (15 ml) at a time, until you get the desired consistency. You want it thick enough to not all run off the bars and thin enough to drizzle. Drizzle over the bars, cut and serve.

TIP

Try to use aluminum-free baking powder as the kind with aluminum can tinge this recipe a bluish hue.

MEYER LEMON CHAMOMILE BARS

I love infusing flavor into baked treats by mingling said flavor with sugar. Lots of chamomile recipes out there have you battling chamomile chunks in the final product, which I don't care for. So, we're going to pulse it together with the sugar until it's reduced to small bits and then strain out any nefarious remaining chamomile chunks. All flavor, no weird texture issues. Pick a chamomile tea that you absolutely love the taste of. You could also mess around with other teas...such as Earl Grey. Let me know how it goes.

MAKES 18 BAR COOKIES

2 cups (272 g) all-purpose flour

⅓ cup (64 g) granulated sugar

¼ cup (38 g) cornstarch

1 tablespoon (9 g) Meyer lemon zest (1 to 2 lemons)

1 teaspoon sea salt

20 tablespoons (287 g) unsalted butter, cut into 20 pieces, room temperature

LEMON FILLING

2 cups (383 g) granulated sugar

2 tablespoons (9 g) loose chamomile tea

4 tablespoons (33 g) powdered sugar

5 large eggs, room temperature

1 large egg yolk, room temperature

¾ cup (177 ml) fresh Meyer lemon juice (4 to 5 lemons)

2 tablespoons (19 g) Meyer lemon zest (2 to 4 lemons)

¾ cup (103 g) all-purpose flour

4 tablespoons (57 g) unsalted butter, cut into 4 pieces, room temperature

¼ cup (33 g) powdered sugar, to garnish

For the crust, preheat your oven to 350°F (177°C). Grease a 9 x 13–inch (23 x 33–cm) casserole dish and line with parchment paper, letting the excess fall over the sides.

In a food processor fitted with the blade attachment, add the flour, sugar, cornstarch, lemon zest and salt in the food processor and pulse several times to mix. Sprinkle the butter over the flour mixture and run the processor for 1 minute, or until a ball starts to form. Press the dough evenly and firmly into the bottom of the prepared casserole dish. Bake in the middle of the oven for 30 minutes or until the edges are lightly bronzed. Set aside to cool completely.

To make the filling, place the granulated sugar and chamomile tea in a food processor and run the machine for 1 to 2 minutes, or until the chamomile is reduced to small flecks. Add in the powdered sugar, eggs, egg yolk, Meyer lemon juice and Meyer lemon zest, and run the machine for 1 minute more or until combined. Add in the flour and run the machine for 15 to 30 seconds.

Strain the mixture into a heavy-bottomed medium saucepan over medium heat. Add the butter and whisk for 6 to 8 minutes or until thickened. If any lumps developed, strain one more time before pouring over the cooled crust. Bake for 15 minutes in the center of the oven. Let the bars cool and then cover and place in the fridge for several hours to set completely.

Pull the bars out of the pan using the excess parchment paper and set on a cutting board. Sift powdered sugar over the top. Cut into squares, cleaning your knife between cuts.

TIP

You can replace the Meyer lemons with regular lemons, just know that you may need more lemons to get the same amount of juice and the resulting bars will be a little tarter.

STELLA'S THAI LEMONGRASS LIME BARS

When last in Thailand, if we weren't laying on the beach, we were eating all of the noodles. Lemongrass, coconut, mint and lime make such a glorious combination that I couldn't wait to transform this flavor quartet into lemon bar's long-lost cousin. For the lemongrass, trim the bottoms of the stalks, peel off the outer layers and coarsely chop before adding to the food processor. These bars have a bright tropical flavor that will leave you dreaming of bikinis, swim-up bars and coconut suntan lotion.

MAKES 18 BAR COOKIES

2 cups (272 g) all-purpose flour

⅓ cup (64 g) granulated sugar

¼ cup (38 g) cornstarch

¼ cup (26 g) unsweetened shredded coconut

1 tablespoon (9 g) lime zest (about 1 large lime)

1 tablespoon (4 g) fresh mint, finely chopped

1 teaspoon sea salt

20 tablespoons (287 g) unsalted butter, cut into 20 pieces, room temperature

LEMONGRASS FILLING

2 cups (383 g) granulated sugar

¼ cup (34 g) fresh lemongrass, chopped

4 tablespoons (33 g) powdered sugar

5 large eggs, room temperature

1 large egg yolk, room temperature

¾ cup (177 ml) fresh lime juice (4 to 5 limes)

2 tablespoons (19 g) lime zest (2 limes)

¾ cup (103 g) all-purpose flour

1 tablespoon (4 g) fresh whole mint leaves

4 tablespoons (57 g) unsalted butter, cut into 4 pieces, room temperature

¼ cup (33 g) powdered sugar, to garnish

For the crust, preheat your oven to 350°F (177°C). Grease a 9 x 13–inch (23 x 33–cm) casserole dish and line with parchment paper, letting the excess fall over the sides.

In a food processor fitted with the blade attachment, add the flour, sugar, cornstarch, coconut, lime zest, mint and salt and pulse several times to mix. Sprinkle the butter over the flour mixture and run the processor for 1 minute, or until a ball starts to form. Press the dough evenly and firmly into the bottom of the casserole dish. Bake in the middle of the oven for 30 minutes or until the sides are lightly bronzed. Set aside to cool completely.

To make the filling, place the granulated sugar and lemongrass in a food processor and run the machine for 1 to 2 minutes or until the lemongrass is reduced to small bits. Add in the powdered sugar, eggs, egg yolk, lime juice, lime zest and run the machine for 1 minute more or until combined. Add in the flour and mint leaves and run the machine for 15 to 30 seconds. Strain the mixture into a medium heavy-bottomed saucepan over medium heat. Add the butter and whisk for 6 to 8 minutes or until thickened. If it develops any lumps, strain one more time before pouring over the cooled crust.

Bake for 15 minutes in the center of the oven. Let the bars cool and then cover and place in the fridge for several hours to set completely.

Pull the bars out of the pan using the excess parchment paper and set on a cutting board. Sift powdered sugar over the top. Cut into squares, cleaning your knife between cuts.

TIP

Lemongrass can be difficult to find. Simply omit it from the recipe if you can't procure some and these will turn out just fine.

PEACH CARDAMOM CRISP BARS

The combination of fruit and streusel and cookie crust is almost more than I can take...I probably could have written an entire chapter on this magical trio of flavors. A couple of quick notes before you get started. I don't peel the peaches in this. When they're coarsely chopped up you'll never know it. Promise. Lastly, peach season is too damn fleeting, am I right? So, for the rest of the year grab around 1½ pounds (680 g) of frozen peaches and follow the recipe as you would with fresh peaches.

MAKES 15 BAR COOKIES

JAMMY PEACHES

1½ pounds (680 g) peaches (about 4 to 5 ripe peaches), pitted and coarsely chopped

¾ cup (144 g) granulated sugar

4½ tablespoons (67 ml) fresh lemon juice (2 to 4 lemons)

2 tablespoons (19 g) lemon zest (2 lemons)

3 tablespoons (45 ml) water

3 teaspoons (9 g) cornstarch

¾ teaspoon cardamom

COOKIE CRUST

2 cups (272 g) all-purpose flour

⅓ cup (64 g) granulated sugar

¼ cup (38 g) cornstarch

1 teaspoon sea salt

20 tablespoons (287 g) unsalted butter, cut into 20 pieces, room temperature

STREUSEL

⅓ cup (45 g) all-purpose flour

4 tablespoons (55 g) light brown sugar, packed

1½ tablespoons (16 g) fine cornmeal

½ teaspoon cinnamon

½ teaspoon cardamom

⅛ teaspoon sea salt

3 tablespoons (43 g) unsalted butter, cold and cut into small pieces

3 tablespoons (23 g) pecans, finely chopped

3 tablespoons (18 g) old-fashioned rolled oats

¼ cup (33 g) powdered sugar, to garnish

To make the jammy peaches, add the peaches, sugar, lemon juice, lemon zest, water, cornstarch and cardamom to a medium saucepan over high heat, stirring to blend. Bring to a boil and then reduce to a simmer for 20 to 25 minutes or until thickened. The jam will continue to thicken as it cools. Set aside to cool completely before assembling the bars. Refrigerate if it needs help firming up a bit.

Preheat the oven to 350°F (177°C). Grease an 8 x 11–inch (20.3- x 28–cm) baking dish and line with parchment paper, letting the excess fall over the sides. To make the crust, in a food processor fitted with the blade attachment, pulse the flour, sugar, cornstarch and sea salt several times to blend. Sprinkle the butter over the flour mixture and run the processor for 1 minute or until a ball forms. Press the mixture evenly into the bottom of the prepared dish and bake in the center of the oven for 30 minutes. Let cool completely. Increase the oven to 375°F (190°C) and place a rack in the top third of the oven.

To make the streusel, in a food processor fitted with the blade attachment, pulse the flour, brown sugar, cornmeal, cinnamon, cardamom and sea salt several times to blend. Sprinkle the butter over the top and pulse until the mixture resembles wet sand. Sprinkle with the pecans and oats and pulse three more times to evenly distribute throughout the streusel. Pinch the streusel to form clumps and place in the fridge to chill.

Once the crust is cooled, spread the jammy peaches over the top and then sprinkle with the streusel, pinching the streusel as you drop it over the top, leaving a gutter around the edge that still shows the peaches. Bake for 30 minutes in the top third of the oven. Let cool completely. Sift powdered sugar over the top.

When ready to serve, use the parchment overhang to pull the cookies from the pan, and with a sharp knife cut into squares, cleaning the knife between cuts. Nobody will complain if you serve with ice cream.

CHOCOLATE ESPRESSO CREAM BARS

This recipe is 100 percent inspired by the chocolate cream pie at the Farmhouse in St. Helena. I don't know where to start...the crust? Heaven. The filling? Next time you're craving chocolate pudding, just make this. And the Espresso Whipped Cream??? Are you even kidding me? This is one of those treats that I have ZERO self-control with and could eat the entire thing myself.

MAKES 15 BAR COOKIES

16 whole chocolate graham crackers (about 9 oz [250 g])

1 cup (132 g) raw hazelnuts, coarsely chopped

4 tablespoons (55 g) dark or light brown sugar, packed

½ teaspoon sea salt

10 tablespoons (143 g) unsalted butter, melted

CHOCOLATE ESPRESSO FILLING

½ cup (96 g) granulated sugar

⅓ cup (51 g) cornstarch

⅓ cup (28 g) unsweetened cocoa powder

½ teaspoon sea salt

5 large egg yolks, room temperature

2 tablespoons (30 ml) freshly brewed espresso, or strong coffee

2 cups (473 ml) milk

¼ cup (1 oz) semisweet chocolate, finely chopped

3 tablespoons (43 g) unsalted butter, cut into 3 pieces, room temperature

ESPRESSO WHIPPED CREAM

1 cup (237 ml) heavy whipping cream, cold

1 tablespoon (12 g) granulated sugar

1 teaspoon finely ground espresso

¼ cup (30 g) dark chocolate curls, to garnish (use a peeler)

To make the crust, preheat the oven to 350°F (177°C) and grease an 8 x 11–inch (20.3 x 28–cm) baking pan and line with parchment paper. If you have cooking spray, spray the top of the parchment paper to help it lay flat against the pan.

Put the graham crackers, hazelnuts, brown sugar and sea salt in a food processor fitted with the blade attachment and run the machine until the mixture becomes a very fine crumb, about 20 pulses. Drizzle the melted butter over the top and pulse until just mixed and it resembles wet sand. Press firmly into the bottom of the prepared baking pan and place the crust in the center of the oven for 10 minutes. Set aside to cool.

To make the filling, in a medium bowl, stir together the sugar, cornstarch, cocoa powder and sea salt. Add in the egg yolks and stir to combine. Slowly stir in the espresso.

In a medium, heavy-bottomed saucepan warm the milk over medium heat. Add ½ cup (118 ml) of the warm milk to the sugar mixture, whisking until combined. Whisk the mixture back into the saucepan, taking care to scrape everything in. Continue whisking for 9 to 10 minutes or until the mixture thickens. Once it's thickened, take it off of the heat and stir in the chocolate and the butter, continuing to stir until smooth. Put some plastic wrap directly over the top of the filling and chill for 1 to 2 hours in the fridge. Once cool, smear evenly over the top of the crust. Cover once again and set in the fridge for several hours more or until chilled through.

To make the whipped cream, place the cold, heavy whipping cream in the bowl of an electric stand mixer fitted with the whisk attachment. Whisk on medium until soft peaks form. Sprinkle the sugar over the top and whisk until soft peaks return, taking care not to overbeat the cream. Sprinkle in the espresso grounds and whisk until combined and it's holding stiff peaks. I prefer the whipped cream added within several hours of serving.

Smear the whipped cream over the top using the back of a spoon to make peaks and valleys, and then sprinkle with shaved chocolate curls. Use the parchment overhang to pull the bars from the pan. Grab a sharp knife to cut into squares, cleaning with a damp paper towel between cuts to get the cleanest cut possible.

CHAI OATMEAL BARS WITH VANILLA BEAN DRIZZLE

I love this recipe because the ingredients are pretty basic stuff that we have in our cupboards and fridge, but the resulting cookie is something extraordinary...a little bit more than just your average oatmeal bar. The one decadent ingredient is the vanilla bean, but feel free to sub in 1 teaspoon of vanilla bean paste or extract.

MAKES 15 BAR COOKIES

8 tablespoons (115 g) unsalted butter, room temperature

1 cup (210 g) light brown sugar, packed

½ cup (96 g) granulated sugar

3 large eggs, room temperature

½ cup (118 ml) sunflower seed oil or other neutral oil

1 tablespoon (15 ml) pure vanilla extract

1¾ cups (238 g) bread flour

¼ cup (34 g) all-purpose flour

1½ teaspoons (4 g) cinnamon

1 teaspoon baking powder

1 teaspoon baking soda

1 teaspoon sea salt

1 teaspoon cardamom

1 teaspoon ground ginger

½ teaspoon freshly grated nutmeg

½ teaspoon cloves

3 cups (273 g) old-fashioned rolled oats

2 cups (292 g) raisins (I like the dark ones)

GLAZE

¾ cup (98 g) powdered sugar

2 tablespoons (30 ml) milk, or more to thin

½ vanilla bean, split and seeds scraped

Preheat your oven to 375°F (190°C). Grease an 8 x 11–inch (20.3 x 28–cm) casserole dish and line with parchment paper, letting the excess hang over the sides.

In an electric stand mixer fitted with the paddle attachment, blend the butter, brown sugar and granulated sugar on medium for 4 minutes or until light and fluffy. With the mixer on low add in the eggs, one at a time, making sure each is blended before adding in the next. Then mix in the oil and vanilla. Scrape down the sides and bottom of the bowl to make sure everything is incorporated. Take the bowl out of the stand mixer.

In a medium bowl, whisk together the bread flour, all-purpose flour, cinnamon, baking powder, baking soda, sea salt, cardamom, ginger, nutmeg and cloves. Stir this into the butter mixture, stopping when you still see streaks of flour. Add in the oats and raisins and stir until distributed throughout. Spoon evenly into the prepared dish and bake for 25 minutes or until the edges are bronzed and the center is puffed up. It will seem slightly underdone, and if tested with a toothpick some small clingy crumbs will come out. Let cool completely before cutting.

To make the glaze, in a small bowl whisk together the powdered sugar, milk and vanilla bean seeds. Add more milk, in 1 teaspoon increments, to get the desired consistency. You want it thick enough to stay on the bars and thin enough so that it falls from the spoon. Drizzle it over the top of the cooled bars all Jackson Pollock–like.

LOADED ROCKY ROAD CARAMEL CRUNCH BARS

You haven't lived until you've eaten these bars. They're basically my fantasy bar loaded with everything delicious in the world: chocolate, caramel, puffed rice, almond slivers and one of the greatest creations of our time—mini marshmallows. What makes them even more compelling is that they are one of the easiest bar cookies out there: mix, pour, bake and eat. Done.

MAKES 15 BAR COOKIES

8 tablespoons (115 g) unsalted butter, room temperature

¾ cup (158 g) light brown sugar, packed

¾ cup (144 g) granulated sugar

2 large eggs, room temperature

⅓ cup (79 ml) sunflower seed oil or other neutral oil

2 tablespoons (30 ml) milk

2 teaspoons (11 ml) real vanilla extract

1½ cups (204 g) bread flour

1 cup (136 g) all-purpose flour

½ cup (43 g) unsweetened dark (Dutch process) cocoa powder

1 teaspoon sea salt

1 teaspoon baking powder

½ teaspoon baking soda

2½ cups (125 g) miniature marshmallows, divided

1½ cups (269 g) semisweet chocolate chips, divided

1 cup (21 g) puffed rice

¾ cup (120 g) almond slivers, divided

1 cup (165 g) soft caramel candy squares, halved (about 14 small caramels)

Preheat your oven to 350°F (177°C) and place a rack in the top third of the oven at least 6 inches (15 cm) from the heat source. Grease an 8 x 11-inch (20.3 x 28–cm) casserole dish and line with parchment paper letting the excess fall over the sides.

In an electric stand mixer fitted with the paddle attachment, add the butter, brown sugar and granulated sugar and mix on medium for 4 minutes, or until light and fluffy. Add in the eggs, one at a time, mixing fully before adding the next. Scrape the sides and bottom of the bowl to make sure everything is incorporated. Add in the oil, milk and vanilla and mix for 1 minute more. Take the bowl out of the stand mixer and set aside.

In a medium bowl, whisk together the bread flour, all-purpose flour, cocoa powder, sea salt, baking powder and baking soda. Add to the butter mixture and stir until blended but you still see streaks of flour. Fold in 2 cups (100 g) of marshmallows, 1¼ cups (224 g) of chocolate chips, the puffed rice and ½ cup (80 g) of almond slivers until evenly distributed. Put half of the batter on the bottom of the prepared casserole dish and sprinkle with the caramel halves. Cover with the remaining dough. Sprinkle the top with the remaining ½ cup (25 g) of mini marshmallows, ¼ cup (45 g) of chocolate chips and ¼ cup (40 g) of almond slivers. With damp hands, gently press the dough into the corners of the pan and smooth out the top a bit.

Bake in the top third of the oven for 20 minutes. Let cool completely in the pan; it may take several hours. Use the excess parchment paper to lift the bars out of the pan and cut with a sharp knife, cleaning the knife with a damp cloth between cuts. These are so good. You're gonna die.

PUMPKIN SPICE BARS
WITH TOASTED MERINGUE

You're in for a treat. These bars are light and spiced and would be perfect without the meringue but are spectacular with it. If you're looking for a reason to buy a kitchen torch, do it now. Meringue always looks better when torched and it is hella good fun.

MAKES 15 BAR COOKIES

12 tablespoons (172 g) unsalted butter, melted

1 cup (237 ml) pumpkin puree (not pumpkin pie filling)

1 cup (210 g) light brown sugar, packed

½ cup (96 g) granulated sugar

½ cup (118 ml) water

3 large eggs, room temperature

2 teaspoons (11 ml) real vanilla extract

1¾ cups (238 g) all-purpose flour

2 teaspoons (5 g) cinnamon

1½ teaspoons (6 g) baking powder

1 teaspoon baking soda

1 teaspoon sea salt

½ teaspoon allspice

½ teaspoon fresh nutmeg

¼ teaspoon ginger

¼ teaspoon cloves

MERINGUE

3 large egg whites, room temperature

¼ teaspoon cream of tartar

¼ teaspoon sea salt

⅔ cup (128 g) granulated sugar

½ teaspoon real vanilla extract

Preheat your oven to 375°F (190°C). Grease an 8 x 11–inch (20.3 x 28–cm) baking pan and line with parchment, letting the excess fall over the sides.

In a large bowl, mix together the butter, pumpkin puree, brown sugar, granulated sugar, water, eggs and vanilla until well blended.

In a small bowl, whisk together the flour, cinnamon, baking powder, baking soda, salt, allspice, nutmeg, ginger and cloves. Pour the flour mixture into the butter mixture and stir until just combined. Spoon the batter into the prepared baking pan and smooth the top with the back of the spoon.

Bake for 35 to 40 minutes on the center rack. Let cool completely in the pan.

To make the meringue, in an electric stand mixer fitted with the whisk attachment, add the egg whites, cream of tartar and salt. Make sure the bowl and whisk are freshly cleaned and dried. Whisk on medium until the eggs are frothy and then slowly add in the granulated sugar. Turn the mixer on high and when the meringue is shiny and glossy and looks like marshmallow fluff, add in the vanilla. Turn the mixer back on high until you reach stiff peaks, which should be just 1 minute more. The meringue will look glossy and hold its shape when you invert the whisk. It should also feel smooth when you rub some between your fingers. Mound the meringue on top of the pumpkin bars using the back of a large spoon to make peaks and valleys. Grab a torch and move it in small circles as you bronze the meringue. If you don't have a torch you could place it underneath the broiler, no closer than 8 inches (20.3 cm) from the heat source. Watch closely and pull it out once the tips are nicely bronzed, making sure the parchment doesn't get torched.

Grab the excess parchment paper to lift the bars out of the pan and onto a cutting board. Cut into squares and serve. Clean the knife with a damp cloth between cuts.

CARROT CAKE BARS

Okay, I think I warned you that some of the bar cookies might be flirting with the idea of also being snack cakes? But some lines were meant to be fuzzy. This recipe will convert even the staunchest carrot cake hater (who even are these people?). This is pure decadence that would be mighty fine on a Thursday as it would to cap off a Friday evening dinner with friends. I absolutely love adding nuts (all kinds of nuts) to baked goods, but I realize it's a very divisive move (as are raisins in carrot anything)...feel free to omit if it ruffles your feathers.

MAKES 18 BAR COOKIES

8 tablespoons (115 g) unsalted butter, room temperature

1 cup (210 g) light brown sugar, packed

½ cup (96 g) granulated sugar

2 large eggs, room temperature

¾ cup (177 ml) sunflower seed oil or other neutral oil

3 teaspoons (15 ml) real vanilla extract

1¾ cups (238 g) bread flour

1 cup plus 1 tablespoon (144 g) all-purpose flour, divided

2 teaspoons (5 g) cinnamon

2 teaspoons (7 g) baking powder

1 teaspoon baking soda

1 teaspoon sea salt

¼ teaspoon freshly grated nutmeg

3½ cups (346 g) carrots, peeled and grated (about 6 medium carrots)

1 cup (146 g) raisins

1 cup (116 g) walnuts, toasted and finely chopped

CRÈME FRAÎCHE FROSTING

7½ ounces (213 g) crème fraîche, room temperature

5 cups (650 g) powdered sugar

½ cup (60 g) candied ginger, finely chopped

Preheat your oven to 350°F (177°C). Grease a 9 x 13–inch (23 x 33–cm) casserole dish and line with parchment paper, letting the excess fall over the sides of the dish.

In an electric stand mixer fitted with the paddle attachment, add the butter, brown sugar and granulated sugar and mix on medium until smooth. Add in the eggs, one at a time, blending completely before adding the next. Be sure to scrape down the sides and bottom of the bowl so that everything is incorporated. Add in the oil and vanilla and run the mixer for 1 minute more. The mixture will be thick and sludge-like. Remove the bowl from the mixer and set aside.

In a medium bowl, whisk together the bread flour, 1 cup (136 g) of all-purpose flour, cinnamon, baking powder, baking soda, salt and nutmeg. Pour this into the butter mixture and stir until just barely combined.

In another medium bowl, stir together the remaining 1 tablespoon (8 g) of flour with the carrots, raisins and walnuts. Fold this into the dough, making sure the carrots, raisins and walnuts are evenly distributed. Pour the mixture into the prepared casserole dish using the back of a spatula to smooth the top a bit. The mixture will be thick.

Bake in the center of the oven for 40 to 45 minutes or until a toothpick pressed in the center of the pan comes out clean. Set the pan on a rack to cool completely. Once cool, use the excess parchment paper to remove the cookies from the pan and place on a cutting board.

To make the frosting, in a medium bowl, whisk together the crème fraîche and powdered sugar. If necessary, add some milk, in 1 teaspoon increments, to thin the frosting. Fold in the candied ginger and smear over the top of the bars. Use a sharp knife to cut into squares.

> **TIP**
> Feel free to sub in cream cheese if you can't find or be bothered with the crème fraîche!

BOOZY BROWN BUTTER BLONDIES

Blondies are sacred ground in our house. Gavin's obsessed with them, and they're one of the sweet treats that I have zero self-control around. I first started futzing with them when we lived in Beijing, and I honed my recipe while living in our current location in California. Blondies by nature have lots of caramel notes. I have us brown the butter to amp this up even more. The bourbon provides some good warmth without being too boozy, while the chocolate chips and pecans give this girl mega personality.

MAKES 15 BLONDIES

16 tablespoons (230 g) unsalted butter

1 cup (210 g) light or dark brown sugar, packed

¾ cup (144 g) granulated sugar

3 large eggs, room temperature

1 tablespoon (15 ml) bourbon

3 teaspoons (15 ml) real vanilla extract

2 cups (272 g) all-purpose flour

1½ teaspoons (7 g) sea salt

1 teaspoon baking powder

1½ cups (180 g) dark chocolate chips

¾ cup (91 g) raw pecans, toasted and coarsely chopped

Preheat the oven to 350°F (177°C). Grease an 8 x 11–inch (20.3 x 28–cm) casserole dish and line with parchment paper, letting the excess fall over the sides.

Put the butter in a small sauce pan and melt over medium heat. Once melted, crank up the heat to medium high. Continue stirring for 2 to 3 minutes and look for small golden bits that will start to settle on the bottom of the pan and it will smell deliciously nutty and caramel-ish. This should take around 3 to 5 minutes total. Once this happens, take it off the heat and pour into a medium, heat-safe bowl to cool for a minute or two. Mix in the brown sugar and granulated sugar and then the eggs, one at a time, making sure each is well blended before adding in the next. Add in the bourbon and vanilla, stirring to combine.

In a medium bowl, whisk together the flour, salt and baking powder. Add this to the butter mixture and stir until almost combined, but you still see streaks of flour. Add in the chocolate chips and pecans, stirring to evenly distribute throughout. Pour into the prepared pan. Smooth it out with the back of your spatula so it's smooth. Bake for about 25 minutes in the middle of the oven. It should start to get a bit of a tan and a hair darker around the edges with only a tiny jiggle in the center. A toothpick inserted into the middle will be lightly coated in cookie dough. Cool completely in the pan (seriously).

When it's time to cut the blondies, use the parchment overhang to remove the blondies from the pan. Grab a very sharp knife and cut straight up and down using a wet paper towel to clean off the knife in between cuts.

> **TIP**
> - If you don't want to add in the booze, feel free to substitute milk or espresso or strong coffee in its place.
> - If you use a larger or smaller pan, be sure to adjust your bake time accordingly. Additionally, these were tested in ceramic pans. Note, if you use a metal pan check earlier for doneness as it could affect the bake time.

GAVIN'S SALTED CARAMEL BLONDIES

These are probably the sweet that Gavin requests the most for school birthdays, special treats or just a basic Wednesday afternoon craving. These get a shiny crackly crust, layers of flavors and I will never, EVER say no to salted caramel. You'll have extra caramel sauce from the recipe below. Make sure you grab some vanilla ice cream the next time you go to the store.

MAKES 15 BLONDIES

SALTED CARAMEL

12 tablespoons (172 g) unsalted butter

1 cup (210 g) dark brown sugar, packed

⅔ cup (158 ml) heavy whipping cream

1 teaspoon real vanilla extract

½ teaspoon sea salt

BLONDIES

16 tablespoons (230 g) unsalted butter

1 cup (210 g) light or dark brown sugar, packed

¾ cup (144 g) granulated sugar

3 large eggs, room temperature

1 tablespoon (15 g) fresh brewed espresso or strong coffee

3 teaspoons (15 ml) real vanilla extract

2 cups (272 g) all-purpose flour

1½ teaspoons (7 g) sea salt

1 teaspoon baking powder

1½ cups (180 g) dark chocolate chips

¾ cup (91 g) raw pecans, toasted and coarsely chopped

¼ cup (60 ml) salted caramel sauce (see above)

To make the caramel, add the butter and brown sugar to a medium saucepan over medium heat and whisk until the sugar is dissolved. Pour in the heavy cream, turn up the heat to medium high and continue whisking until it reaches a boil, and then reduce the heat to medium for about 5 minutes or until thickened. Stir in the vanilla and sea salt and set aside to cool, whisking frequently. If it starts to separate, whisk it until it's completely blended once again. Once cool, place it in a covered container and refrigerate until ready to use.

To make the blondies, preheat the oven to 350°F (177°C). Grease an 8 x 11–inch (20.3 x 28–cm) baking dish and line with parchment paper, letting the excess fall over the sides.

Put the butter in a small sauce pan and melt over medium heat. Once melted, crank up the heat to medium high. Continue stirring for 2 to 3 minutes and look for small golden bits that will start to settle on the bottom of the pan and it will smell deliciously nutty and caramel-y. This should take around 3 to 5 minutes total. Once this happens, take it off the heat and pour it into a medium, heat-safe bowl to cool for a minute or two. Mix in the brown sugar, granulated sugar and eggs, one at a time, making sure each is well blended before adding in the next. Add in the coffee and vanilla, stirring to combine.

In a medium bowl, whisk together the flour, salt and baking powder. Add this to the butter mixture and stir until almost combined, but you still see streaks of flour. Add in the chocolate chips and pecans, stirring to evenly distribute throughout. Pour this into the prepared pan. Smooth the top with the back of your spatula so it's even. Drizzle ¼ cup (60 ml) of the caramel over the top, using a knife to swirl it about. Reserve leftover caramel for another use.

Bake for about 25 to 30 minutes in the middle of the oven. It should start to get a bit of a tan and a hair darker around the edges with only a tiny jiggle in the center. Cool completely in the pan (seriously).

When it's time to cut the blondies, use the parchment overhang to pull the blondies from the pan. Grab a very sharp knife and cut straight up and down, using a wet paper towel to clean off the knife in between cuts.

OOEY GOOEY FUDGY BROWNIES

I'm obsessed with super fudgy brownies. We're going to melt all of our wet ingredients in a double boiler for two reasons. First, melted chocolate is fussy when blended with other ingredients that aren't the same temperature, and this solves that problem. Second, it gives these brownies that shiny, slightly crispy lid that I'm obsessed with. Plus, it's a pretty pain-free way to make brownies.

MAKES 15 BROWNIES

1½ cups (180 g) dark chocolate, finely chopped

1 cup (192 g) granulated sugar

¾ cup (158 g) light brown sugar, packed

8 tablespoons (115 g) unsalted butter, cut into 8 pieces

⅓ cup (79 ml) sunflower seed oil or other neutral oil

4 large eggs, room temperature

1 tablespoon (15 ml) freshly brewed espresso, or strong coffee

1 tablespoon (15 ml) real vanilla extract

1 cup (136 g) all-purpose flour

⅔ cup (56 g) unsweetened dark (Dutch process) cocoa powder

1 teaspoon sea salt

2 teaspoons (10 g) sea salt flakes, optional

Preheat the oven to 350°F (177°C). Grease an 8 x 11–inch (20.3 x 28–cm) baking dish and line with parchment paper, letting the excess fall over the sides.

In a medium, heat-safe bowl add the chocolate, granulated sugar, brown sugar, butter and oil and set over a medium saucepan of simmering water. Do not let the bowl touch the water or let the water come to a boil. Stir frequently until melted and smooth. Place a towel on the counter and set the bowl on top of it. Whisk in the eggs, one at a time, making sure each is well blended before adding in the next. Add in the espresso and vanilla and stir to combine.

In a small bowl, whisk together the flour, cocoa powder and salt. Add this to the chocolate mixture and stir until just combined. Pour the batter into the prepared baking dish. Use the back of your spoon to even the top a bit. Sprinkle with the sea salt flakes, if using.

Bake on the middle rack of the oven for 25 minutes. When done, they will have a bit of jiggle in the middle, and if you test with a toothpick a wee bit of batter will coat it. This is a good thing. Let them cool in the pan for several hours and if you want super, uber fudgy brownies shove them in the fridge for several hours before serving.

When it's time to cut the brownies, use a very sharp knife, cut straight up and down and use a wet paper towel to clean off the knife in between cuts.

CHOCOLATE RYE ZUCCHINI BARS

When I grow zucchini over the summer months it's seriously a blitzkrieg over here. Squash plants are prolific and I'm always looking for new and interesting ways to cook and bake with them. These bars are the perfect solution. They're so loaded with finely shredded zucchini that they should be considered a veggie serving. Me thinks. And rye and chocolate will forever and always be one of my favorite flavor pairings.

MAKES 15 BAR COOKIES

2 cups (155 g) zucchini, finely shredded (about 2 to 3 small zucchini)

1¼ cups (150 g) dark chocolate, finely chopped

8 tablespoons (115 g) unsalted butter, cut into 8 pieces

¼ cup (55 g) light brown sugar, packed

¼ cup (59 ml) sunflower seed oil or other neutral oil

½ cup (96 g) granulated sugar

3 large eggs, room temperature

1 tablespoon (15 ml) real vanilla extract

½ cup (51 g) dark rye flour

½ cup (68 g) all-purpose flour

⅔ cup (56 g) unsweetened dark (Dutch process) cocoa powder

1 teaspoon baking powder

1 teaspoon sea salt

1½ cups (180 g) dark chocolate, chopped

Sea salt flakes to sprinkle on top, optional

Preheat the oven to 375°F (190°C). Grease an 8 x 11–inch (20.3 x 28–cm) pan and line with parchment paper, letting the excess hang over the sides. Place the shredded zucchini on several layers of paper towels, cover with more paper towels and press out the excess moisture.

In a medium, heat-safe bowl, add the finely chopped chocolate, butter, brown sugar, oil and granulated sugar and set it over a medium saucepan of simmering water. Do not let the bowl touch the water or let the water come to a boil. Stir frequently until melted and smooth. Place a towel on the counter and place the bowl on top of it. Add in the eggs one at a time, making sure each is well blended before adding in the next. Stir in the vanilla and set aside.

In a medium bowl, whisk together the dark rye flour, all-purpose flour, cocoa powder, baking powder and salt. Add to the chocolate mixture and stir until combined. Fold in the shredded zucchini and chopped dark chocolate. Pour the batter into your prepared 8 x 11–inch (20.3 x 28–cm) dish. Use the back of your spoon to even the top a bit and bake in the center of the oven for 35 to 40 minutes. When done, they will have a bit of jiggle in the middle. Let the zucchini bars cool completely, at least 2 to 3 hours, and then refrigerate.

To cut the bars, remove them from the pan using the excess parchment paper and with a very sharp knife, cut them into squares, cleaning your knife with a damp cloth between cuts to get the cleanest cut possible. Sprinkle with sea salt flakes before serving, if using.

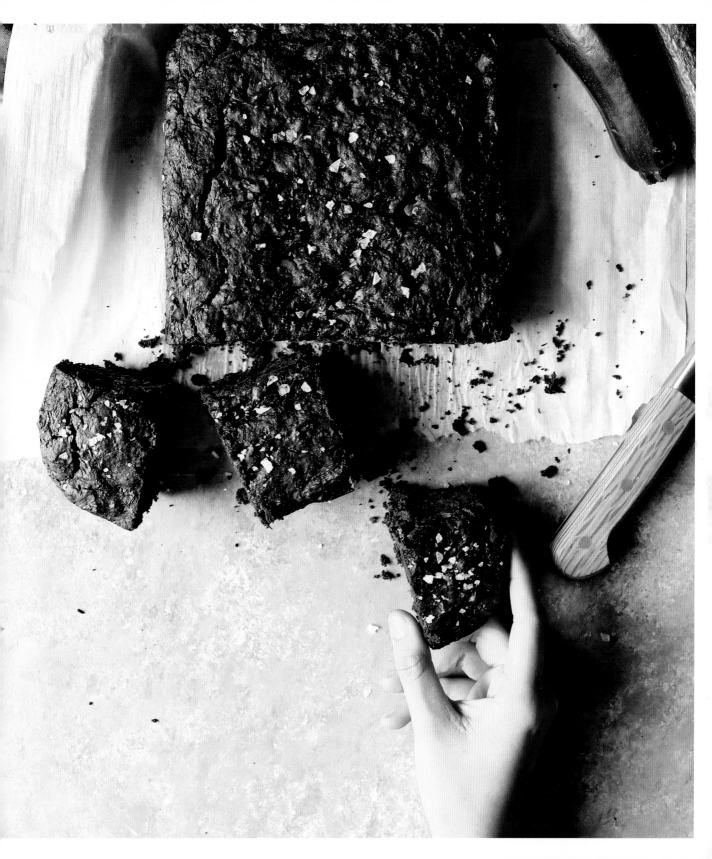

CHERRY STREUSEL JAM BARS
WITH PINK PEPPERCORN COOKIE CRUST

You're going to bookmark this recipe not just because these bars are freaking delicious, but also because you're going to want to make extra jam to smear on top of everything in your kitchen or just eat straight from the jar with a spoon. The cherry jam is scented with almond extract (just like my favorite cherry pie), with that flavor echoed by almond slivers in the streusel. The crust has the consistency of a sandy sugar cookie with just a smidge of spice from the pink peppercorns. And don't let the peppercorns fool you...they're actually a berry that lends the most delicate flavor and color to the crust.

MAKES 15 BAR COOKIES

CHERRY JAM

1 pound (434 g) fresh cherries, pitted and halved

½ cup (96 g) granulated sugar

½ cup (83 g) dried tart cherries

3 tablespoons (45 ml) lemon juice

3 tablespoons (28 g) lemon zest

2 tablespoons (30 ml) water

2 teaspoons (10 ml) almond extract

2 teaspoons (6 g) cornstarch

½ teaspoon cinnamon

COOKIE CRUST

6 tablespoons (72 g) granulated sugar

2 tablespoon (17 g) whole pink peppercorns

2 cups (272 g) all-purpose flour

¼ cup (38 g) cornstarch

1 teaspoon sea salt

20 tablespoons (287 g) unsalted butter, cut into 20 pieces, room temperature

To make the jam, add the fresh cherries, sugar, dried cherries, lemon juice, lemon zest, water, almond extract, cornstarch and cinnamon to a medium saucepan over high heat, stirring to blend. Bring it to a boil and then reduce to a simmer for 5 minutes or until thickened. The jam will continue to thicken as it cools. Set aside to cool completely.

To make the crust, preheat your oven to 350°F (177°C). Grease an 8 x 11–inch (20.3 x 28–cm) casserole dish and line with parchment paper, letting the excess fall over the sides.

In a food processor fitted with the blade attachment, add the sugar and peppercorns and run for 2 to 3 minutes. Sift out and discard any big peppercorn chunks and return the sugar to the food processor.

Place the flour, cornstarch and salt in the food processor and pulse several times to mix. Sprinkle the butter over the flour mixture and run the processor for 1 minute or until a ball forms. Press the dough evenly into the bottom of the casserole dish; it will seem heavily seasoned with peppercorns and excessively buttery...but it's perfect. Bake in the middle of the oven for 30 minutes or until the sides are lightly bronzed. Set aside to cool completely.

(continued)

CHERRY STREUSEL JAM BARS WITH
PINK PEPPERCORN COOKIE CRUST (CONTINUED)

STREUSEL

½ cup (68 g) all-purpose flour

3 tablespoons (41 g) brown sugar, packed

½ teaspoon cinnamon

⅛ teaspoon cardamom

⅛ teaspoon sea salt

4 tablespoons (57 g) unsalted butter, cut into 4 chunks, cold

3 tablespoons (30 g) almond slivers

¼ cup (33 g) powdered sugar, to garnish

To make the streusel, in a small bowl, whisk together the flour, brown sugar, cinnamon, cardamom and sea salt. Using a pastry blender or two forks, work the butter into the mixture until it has the consistency of wet sand. Mix in the almonds. Pinch together to make small clumps throughout the streusel and then stash in the fridge or freezer until ready to use.

Increase the oven to 375°F (190°C).

To assemble, pour the jam evenly on top of the crust and then sprinkle with the streusel. Bake in the center of the oven for 30 minutes until the jam is bubbly and the streusel lightly bronzed.

Once cool, sift the powdered sugar over the top. Use the parchment handles to pull the cookies out of the pan. Grab a sharp knife and cut into squares, cleaning the knife with a damp towel between cuts.

TIPS

· If you decide you can't be bothered with pitting a pound of cherries, feel free to reach for your favorite jam. You'll need about 1½ cups (340 ml) for the filling.

· If you omit the peppercorns there is no need to pulse the sugar by itself.

· The jam and streusel can be made ahead of time and stored in the fridge until use.

ACKNOWLEDGMENTS

I swore this wouldn't sound like an awards speech, but alas I failed. Brace yourself...

First, to all of the readers of DisplacedHousewife.com, without you none of this would have happened. In 2014 when I posted my first recipe I didn't dream that this best-case scenario would come true. I am so grateful for each and every one of you.

To Gavin and Stella, I love you both more than words. Thank you so much for lending your beautiful hands to my photos in the wee morning hours and your completely uncensored food-critic skills.

To my mom and dad, holy crap...thank you for EVERYTHING!!! I'm so thankful for all of your help throughout this entire process.

To Leigh Eisenman, my agent, for believing in me. Maybe we should have known when we had our L.A. Story, agent-talent lunch meeting at the Beverly Hills Hotel (and I gave you a box of Brown Butter Muscovado Snickerdoodles) that our first book would be a cookie book? Thanks Adam and Ryan for the introduction. You guys are the best!

To Marissa Giambelluca, my editor, you have no idea how much your first email meant to me and how I sat, stunned, staring at my computer screen and so completely excited that you were interested in making a book with me. I'd like to bottle up that feeling and dab it behind my ears daily. Thank you for making a dream come true.

To everyone at Page Street, thank you so much for putting time and care into making this book beautiful. Meg Baskis, I absolutely love how clean and elegant you made the pages look. It's been wonderful working with you.

To my awesome, baller crew of testers. I can't thank you guys enough. Christi Lazar you have been my unofficial tester for years (it's been years, right?)...you were destined for this role!! Mary Ann Dwyer, your feedback and notes always put a smile on my face...thank you for the time and care you gave the recipes. To one Miss Natalie Neumann...you, my friend, are my youngest tester but your notes, feedback and questions were on par with those that have been baking for far longer. Keep baking! Hilary Halme, thanks pengyou for testing my recipes and being there for so much more!! Uncle Mike, thanks for your services. I'm glad I've converted you into a bread maker!

Last, but definitely not least, to my friends...I've missed you all while I've been buried in mounds of cookies. By the time you're reading this hopefully we will have resumed wine lunches, nights out in L.A., mid-morning coffees and just face time in general.

One more mega thanks to my mom for suggesting that I submit a recipe to a magazine, which spurred me to start writing a blog, which eventually landed me here. Thank you, thank you, thank you!!

xo

ABOUT THE AUTHOR

Rebecca Firth is a food writer, photographer and creator of the Saveur-nominated blog, DisplacedHousewife.com, where she shares recipes of mostly sweets (and sometimes eats). Her work has appeared both on- and offline in *Bake From Scratch Magazine*, *Bake From Scratch: Volume Two*, *Rachael Ray Every Day*, *Sunset Magazine*, Buzzfeed, *Teen Vogue*, Epicurious, feedfeed, AOL, MSN, *The Huffington Post*, Bread Collection 2018 and more. *The Cookie Book* is her first book.

Rebecca lives in the Santa Ynez Valley, California.

www.displacedhousewife.com

INDEX